CO-ALL-287

Table of Contents

IMPLICATIONS

OF

SOVIET

NEW THINKING

...ley

...etrich Genscher

...t

...Whitehead

Summary Report of
International Conference
St. Paul, Minnesota
October 9-11, 1987

Executive Summary
Report of the Task Force on
Soviet New Thinking

WESTVIEW PRESS ✦ BOULDER, COLORADO

 Institute for East-West Security Studies
New York   1987

Distributed by
Westview Press, Inc.
5500 Central Avenue
Boulder, Colorado 80301

Institute for East-West Security Studies
360 Lexington Avenue, New York, NY 10017

The Institute for East-West Security Studies does not take or encourage specific policy positions. It is committed to encouraging and facilitating discussions of important issues of concern to East and West. The views expressed in this book do not necessarily reflect the opinions of the Board of Directors, the officers or the staff of the Institute.

The printing and distribution of this publication has been made possible through the generous support of Honeywell.

ISBN 0-8133-7736-6 (Westview)

Preface

We are pleased to be able to present some of the important remarks and ideas delivered recently at a major international conference on the "Implications of Soviet New Thinking."

The timing and the importance of the subject matter led to major media coverage of the conference in the world press and a national television audience in the United States on the C-SPAN public television system. That coverage, in turn, has generated widespread interest in a permanent printed record of the discussions held at the St. Paul, Minnesota conference October 9-11, 1987. Major foreign policy speeches delivered by Hans-Dietrich Genscher, long-serving Foreign Minister and Vice Chancellor of the Federal Republic of Germany, U.S. Deputy Secretary of State John Whitehead, Deputy Foreign Minister Harry Ott of the German Democratic Republic, and U.S. Senator Bill Bradley are presented in this volume together with a summary of the conference deliberations.

This report is intended for American and European audiences. The substantive materials contained in this report will serve as a useful point of departure in the debate about the future of East-West relations. What kind of relationship do we wish to have with the other side? If we are truly at a crossroads in East-West relations, what is our agenda for action?

The reader is advised to begin a review of the contents of this publication with the Executive Summary of the Report of the bipartisan Task Force on Soviet New Thinking. The Task Force Report, entitled *How Should America Respond to Gorbachev's Challenge?*, was the result of eight months of work by 38 prominent Americans under the chairmanship of Professor Joseph Nye of Harvard University and Whitney MacMillan of Cargill, Inc. The conference in St. Paul was, to a large degree, a discussion of the spirit and content of that Task Force Report, the first systematic Western public effort to assess and formulate a response to the changes in the Soviet Union brought about by Mikhail Gorbachev.

The contribution of the major speakers was matched by important presentations from panelists including Foreign Ministers Thorvald Stoltenberg of Norway and Steingrimur Hermannsson of Iceland, U.S. Congressmen Tom Downey and Bill Frenzel, former Vice President Walter Mondale, business leaders Don Kendall of PepsiCo, Bob Hormats of Goldman Sachs, Jim Giffen of the U.S.-USSR Trade & Economic Council, syndicated columnists Flora Lewis and William Pfaff, journalists Michel Tatu of *Le Monde*, Edward Mortimer of the *Financial Times*, David Ignatius of *The Washington Post*, and specialists Robert Legvold, Ed Hewett, Bill Luers, Marshall Goldman, Hal Sonnenfeldt, and Dick Ullman.

The quality and diversity of the conference participants further enriched the discussions. The report of the working groups and panels offered some useful ideas to those interested in pursuing the issue of how East and West should proceed in changing their relationship. The Institute is proud to sponsor this publication and is grateful to Honeywell, a multinational corporation based in Minneapolis, Minnesota, for its important financial support which makes this publication possible.

My colleagues Dr. F. Stephen Larrabee, Dr. Allen Lynch and Peter B. Kaufman are responsible for the rapid release of this publication—as well as for its quality. Appreciation is paid to the Institute's staff and research interns who served as rapporteurs during the conference.

The Institute wishes to thank the trustees and staff of Macalester College in St. Paul, in particular its President, Dr. Robert Gavin, for the outstanding hospitality exhibited throughout the conference. We also appreciate the efforts of American Public Radio, Minnesota Public Radio, C-SPAN, National Public Radio, Cable North Central, Hauser Communications, the Associated Press and countless others who were responsible for the widespread media coverage of the conference.

Financial support for this conference was provided by numerous foundations, corporations, and individuals in the Twin Cities. Particular appreciation is paid to Cargill, Inc., the F. R. Bigelow Foundation, Honeywell, 3M Company, the McKnight Foundation and the Carnegie Corporation of New York for their outstanding generosity.

In addition we wish to express appreciation to the City of St. Paul and its Mayor George Latimer, the Federal Reserve Bank of Minneapolis and its President Gary Stern, the *Star Tribune* and its Publisher Roger Parkinson, Norwest Capital Advisers and its President Peter Heegaard, and Whitney and Betty MacMillan of Cargill Inc. for hosting major events during the conference.

The Task Force Report, the conference itself, and this Report represent an enormous effort by the entire staff of the Institute. Special appreciation is paid to Dr. Rhoda Mintzer, Keith Wind, Mary Lane Thompson, Margaret Cosentino and Claire Gordon as well as Mary Albon, Mary Corry, Elizabeth Cristancho, Rosalinda DeVera, Marjorie George, Louise Greif, Michael Gross, Amy Lew, Maria Mercado, Kerry S. McNamara, Rodney Snyder, Natalia Young, Jan Zamoyta of the staff and special conference media consultants Steve Lynch and Peter Mahoney from E. F. Hutton.

The Institute believes that this Report represents an important contribution to the East-West dialogue. We are working to make its contents widely known among the policy and media communities in both East and West. We would like to hear your comments and suggestions. The broader and deeper the debate in both East and West about the future of our relationship, the more likely we are to arrive at some important and far-reaching decisions that will benefit both. This Report is prepared not so much as a record of a conference as it is a contribution to that debate. The Institute will build upon this work in 1988 when an East-West Task Force of Europeans and Americans is launched to further explore an agenda of action for improving the relationship.

> John Edwin Mroz
> President
> Institute for East-West Security Studies
> New York
> November 9, 1987

Introduction

After a long period of deterioration, U.S.-Soviet relations appear to have entered a new, more positive phase. The imminent conclusion of a treaty on intermediate- and short-range nuclear forces and the approach of a third Reagan-Gorbachev summit suggest that both sides may be able to put bilateral relations on a firmer footing and work together to ameliorate some of the causes of tension in recent years. At the same time, the changes in the Soviet Union initiated by General Secretary Mikhail Gorbachev have raised important questions about the prospects for reform in the Soviet Union. How real are these changes? Do they open up new opportunities for Western policy or are they simply cosmetic changes, designed to lure the West into lowering its guard while the Soviet Union strengthens its ability to compete more efficiently with the West? How should the West respond to these changes?

These questions take on even greater relevance with the approach of a third superpower summit. The summit opens up the possibility for establishing a more constructive relationship with the Soviet Union and for addressing the key issues that have divided the two countries in the past. Yet the West, especially the United States, remains unclear about how to respond to many of Gorbachev's initiatives. Many Americans have argued that the United States should take a "wait-and-see" attitude toward Gorbachev, that the best policy would be for the West to wait until the dust has settled in Moscow. This runs the serious risk, however, of letting Gorbachev define the pace and scope of the East-West agenda. There is thus an urgent need for a more informed and coherent policy debate on how the United States and its West European allies should respond to the opportunities and challenges presented by the ongoing changes in the Soviet Union.

With this in mind, the Institute for East-West Security Studies put together a bipartisan Task Force of distinguished Americans from business, academia, and the media. In its Report, *How Should America Respond to Gorbachev's Challenge?*, the Task Force, chaired by Whitney MacMillan, President of Cargill and Co-Chairman of the Institute's Board of Directors, and Professor Joseph Nye, Director of the Center for Science and International Affairs at Harvard University, sought to analyze the changes in the Soviet Union initiated by Gorbachev and their implications for the United States and its West European allies. (The Executive Summary of the Task Force Report is contained in this volume.) While acknowledging that the long-term success of Gorbachev's reforms remains uncertain, the Report concludes that many of the changes move in directions conducive to Western interests and that they require a more active and constructive U.S. policy designed to test Gorbachev on a wide range of issues from arms control to regional conflicts.

The results of the Task Force were presented at a major international conference sponsored by the Institute in St. Paul, Minnesota, October 9-11, 1987. The conference was attended by nearly 350 participants from the United States, Western Europe, and Eastern Europe. The discussions in St. Paul focused on two major issues: (1) the significance of the recent changes in the Soviet Union and (2) how the West, especially the United States, should respond.

The proceedings of the conference contained in this volume highlight several important features of the current East-West debate. First, they suggest that there is a growing, albeit far from complete, consensus within the United States about the significance of the changes undertaken by Gorbachev. When Gorbachev first initiated many of these changes, most Americans, within the government and outside, were highly skeptical about their seriousness and significance. By the time of the conference in St. Paul, however, the debate had clearly shifted. The question was no longer whether Gorbachev is serious but whether he can really succeed in carrying out reform and how the West should react.

Western Policy Options

In his opening remarks to the conference, West German

Foreign Minister Hans-Dietrich Genscher stated that the West has to decide whether to adopt a "wait-and-see" attitude toward developments in the Soviet Union or to begin examining how these developments can be used for the establishment of a new and constructive relationship between East and West. He argued that if a turning point is now at hand, it would be a mistake of historic proportions for the West to miss such an opportunity. A Soviet Union that is adopting a more open domestic and foreign policy, he felt, is a better partner, above all a more predictable partner, for the West than a Soviet Union that seals itself off from the outside world and becomes increasingly hidebound in domestic affairs.

The conference made clear that differing perspectives continue to exist among the United States and its West European allies. Representing the Reagan administration, Deputy Secretary of State John Whitehead took a more cautious approach in his speech at the conference. He put emphasis on the need for "clear thinking" rather than "new thinking." Much of what is exciting in U.S.-Soviet relations, he argued, could be seen as a Soviet response to America's challenge that the USSR become a peaceful, constructive participant in the affairs of the modern world. He credited the recent progress in U.S.-Soviet relations more to the administration's steady pursuit of its central objectives in four key areas—human rights, arms control, regional conflicts, and bilateral issues—than to Soviet "new thinking." While acknowledging recent changes in Soviet human rights behavior, he warned that the West would be in a better position to elicit increased Soviet respect for human rights if it avoided being "entranced" by the novelty of what was happening in the Soviet Union and kept in mind how much distance remained to be covered.

Another cautious note was struck by Senator Bill Bradley in his keynote speech to the conference. While welcoming many of the recent changes, he noted that signs of a thaw in U.S.-Soviet relations had occurred before—in 1955 and 1968—only to be proven premature. Many Americans hope that Gorbachev's reforms might bring about a real turning point in U.S.-Soviet relations. But hope, he argued, is not enough. The West cannot ignore the fact that many of the issues that have troubled America's relationship with the Soviet Union in the past have remained unchanged. At the same time, he argued, the United

States has to be flexible enough to seize new opportunities and have "antennae sensitive enough to hear the soft inner voice" of the Soviet Union as well as to discern threats.

The conference also demonstrated that a unified West European consensus has yet to emerge. While many West German and Scandinavian participants tended to share Foreign Minister Genscher's view that the West should hold Gorbachev to his word and test the Soviet leader, the British and French representatives took a more reserved and skeptical view of both the degree of change and its importance. The problem, as David Gore-Booth, Head of the Policy Planning Staff of the British Foreign Office, pointed out, is that the West Europeans are "both behind and in front of the Americans." They are "in front" in recommending the exploration of prospects for specific changes in Soviet policy—especially in the Middle East and Eastern Europe—and "behind" by showing more caution in their overall judgment.

New Thinking and Eastern Europe

The new thinking is not simply a U.S.-Soviet or alliance issue. It has important implications for Moscow's East European allies as well. Here too the reaction to Gorbachev's efforts at reform has been nuanced and differentiated, with some East European countries welcoming the changes and others taking a more reserved stand about some aspects. For Moscow's allies in Eastern Europe, as the conference made clear, the key issue is not the changes themselves—which all East European countries in principle support—but their applicability to individual East European countries. Just as there is no one model of socialism that is universally valid, there is also no one model of reform that is suited to all East European countries. What works in the Soviet Union may not necessarily be applicable in Eastern Europe, in countries which have different cultural and political traditions as well as different levels of economic development.

Under Gorbachev, Moscow's allies in Eastern Europe have been given greater latitude to pursue their own national interests and to develop their own variety of socialism. As Gorbachev noted in his speech to the foreign delegates during the celebration of the seventieth anniversary of the Bolshevik Revolution in

Moscow in early November, "Unity does not mean identity and uniformity." Moscow, he emphasized, believes that there is "no model of socialism to be emulated by everyone." Elsewhere Gorbachev has called for a "more sophisticated culture of relations," one which recognizes the diversity within Eastern Europe and the contribution which individual socialist states can make to strengthening the socialist community and enhancing detente.

This last point was emphasized in particular by Harry Ott, Deputy Foreign Minister and the Permanent Representative of the German Democratic Republic to the United Nations, in his speech to the conference. The GDR, he noted, has a special responsibility for reducing confrontation which stems from its bitter experience in two world wars that began from German territory, and from the fact that the GDR is on the dividing line between the two most powerful military alliances. These experiences require the GDR to do everything possible to ensure that war never again emanates from German soil. The recent visit of GDR party leader Erich Honecker to West Germany, he emphasized, is an important reflection of the GDR's desire to contribute to greater stability and security in Europe.

Arms Control

Arms control issues remain at the core of U.S.-Soviet relations. Yet as the proceedings in Minnesota underscored, there continue to be different perspectives between the United States and its West European allies as well as among the allies themselves about many arms control issues. Many of these differences centered around the INF agreement expected to be signed at the upcoming summit. While America's West European allies formally support the agreement, the concerns among non-government specialists about its long-term implications were clearly visible in St. Paul. Some West Europeans fear that it may be the first step toward the "denuclearization" of Europe. Others worry about its impact on NATO's strategy of "flexible response" and the credibility of the American nuclear deterrent. A significant reduction of medium- and short-range nuclear missiles, moreover, will make efforts to redress the conventional balance even more urgent. Indeed, many West Europeans see

Gorbachev's stated willingness to redress existing conventional imbalances as the main gauge of his seriousness about arms control.

While the Soviet Union has shown little interest in conventional arms control in the past, under Gorbachev the Soviet position on conventional arms control has begun to change and Moscow has recently displayed a new readiness, at least rhetorically, to address a number of key Western concerns. Among the most important recent significant changes have been:

- Gorbachev's willingness to admit the existence of force "asymmetries";

- a new emphasis in authoritative Soviet and Warsaw Treaty Organization statements on the need to constrain offensive capabilities and eliminate the capacity for "surprise attack";

- proposals for the creation of nuclear-free zones and corridors;

- a call for a dialogue on military doctrines; and

- the introduction of the concept of "reasonable sufficiency" as a criterion for force planning.

Some Soviet civilian analysts have also begun to reexamine the historical importance of conventional defense and to challenge the long-standing notion in Soviet military thought that a decisive offensive attack is the key to victory. To be sure, at present these changes are largely rhetorical and it remains to be seen how and to what degree they will be implemented in practice. Yet, as a number of conference participants stressed, these changes should not be dismissed lightly. Taken together with economic pressures and advances in Western technology (precision-guided missiles, "smart weapons," etc.), they could give the Soviet Union greater incentive to take conventional arms control seriously in the future. A large number of Western participants at the conference believed, however, that getting the Soviet military to accept these changes will not be easy.

In addition, there are a number of concrete obstacles to rapid progress in conventional arms control. The most important include:

1. *The role of nuclear elements.* The East wants to see nuclear

elements, especially battlefield nuclear weapons, included in any discussions on conventional reductions. The problem of whether to include nuclear elements is most acute for the Federal Republic. Many West Germans would like to see a reduction of shorter-range nuclear weapons (under 500 kilometers), especially nuclear artillery, since these weapons, once fired, would hit West German territory, killing West Germans. Few, however, want to see a total elimination of nuclear weapons (the so-called "triple zero solution"). Even if conventional forces are significantly reduced, they argue, for the forseeable future the West will need to maintain some capacity for a nuclear response.

2. *Size of the reductions.* A second point of disagreement is over the size of reductions. While East and West agree in principle on the need for asymmetrical reductions, there is little agreement on the magnitude of cuts required or what exactly should be cut. Indeed, the "data issue," the old bug-a-boo of the MBFR talks, quickly reemerged at the conference, with many Eastern participants claiming that there exists a rough conventional balance and Western observers hotly disputing these claims. In short, a change in forum and enlargement of the number of states involved is not likely to resolve deep-seated structural problems and differences in approach between the two sides. Indeed, in many ways, enlarging the forum may complicate the negotiations and make these differences more difficult to resolve.

3. *Verification.* Any new conventional arms control agreement, as Western conference participants pointed out, will need to contain adequate provisions for verification, including the right of on-site "challenge" inspections. Even then it will be very difficult to verify manpower reductions with great accuracy. This issue is likely to prove to be one of the most difficult and contentious in the negotiations.

4. *Military doctrine.* The East has proposed discussions on military doctrine. As the discussions in St. Paul made clear, many Western observers are skeptical about the usefulness of such a dialogue, fearing that it will be used by the Soviet Union as a propaganda forum to attack NATO policy. Others, however, feel that such a dialogue could help to clarify perceptions. They argue that the West could turn the forum to its own advantage by pointing to evidence of the Soviet Union's offensive posture

and doctrine in Soviet military literature and military exercises.

These differences suggest that any progress in conventional arms control is likely to be slow and difficult. In some cases, unilateral steps may prove more productive than negotiated measures. The discussions in St. Paul also suggested that it may be useful to look more seriously at possible tradeoffs. A number of participants, for instance, argued that the West should consider trading some of its tactical nuclear artillery for a sharp reduction in Soviet tanks. This proposal was strongly opposed by several representatives from NATO countries, however, indicating that there is far from a unified view in the West on how best to proceed.

The Economic Dimension

The most far-reaching changes undertaken by Gorbachev have been in the economic realm. Yet, as the discussions in St. Paul made clear, many Western observers doubt that Gorbachev can ultimately achieve his goals without further changes in public attitudes and the economic system itself. Opposition, both active and passive, to radical reform remains strong, as underscored by the unexpected resignation of Boris Yeltsin, the boss of the Moscow party district and one of Gorbachev's closest allies, after the party plenum in late October. As Robert Hormats, Vice Chairman of Goldman Sachs, pointed out, one reason that the Chinese reforms have taken root to the degree that they have is that the political and economic disruptions of the Cultural Revolution convinced most Chinese that a new and dramatically different course was necessary. In contrast, many Soviet citizens feel relatively secure with the current economic structure in the USSR.

Other obstacles also give reason for skepticism. There remains an inherent contradiction, for instance, between Gorbachev's desire to give factory managers and enterprises more authority for day-to-day decisions and the imperatives of a still largely centralized system that fixes the prices on major factory inputs and constantly imposes regulatory and output requirements from above. Moreover, greater autonomy for such organizations will inevitably mean a reduced role for the party and state bureaucracy in everyday economic management. Will these institutions really be willing to accept such a diminution of their power and influence?

Finally, there is the linkage between economic reform and political reform. As the Czechoslovak experience in 1967-1968 and the more recent Hungarian experience illustrate, efforts to decentralize economic decision-making require changes in the political arena. Particularly vital are a more open exchange of information among universities, industry, and the scientific community and greater contact with institutions abroad. This will pose difficulties for a system that has traditionally been highly compartmentalized and relatively closed to outside influences. In the short term, however, the major obstacle to reform in the Soviet Union is likely to be the lack of trained managers capable of taking initiative under the new, more flexible system. As a result, the benefits of reform are likely to be slow.

In the debates over how the West should respond to Gorbachev's economic reforms, several schools of thought can be distinguished. One argues that the United States and its allies should have as little trade as possible with the Soviet Union, since such trade would only serve to strengthen Soviet "aggressiveness" and allow Moscow to avoid reforms that it would otherwise be forced to undertake. This view found few supporters in St. Paul. Many agreed with Iceland's Foreign Minister Steingrimur Hermannsson, who argued in his speech at the conference that an economically backward country which has the power to destroy the world is a much greater threat to mankind than one which is prospering and whose people are content.

A second group does not oppose trade per se but believes that it should be part of an overall political strategy designed to encourage reform. Senator Bradley, for instance, argued that trade should be seen as a "strategic asset" and that the West should attach conditions to any flow of capital eastward. This view was hotly contested by Donald Kendall, Chairman and Chief Executive Officer of Pepsico, who questioned whether it would be possible or even desirable to impose such political controls. Such controls, he argued, are not only unworkable but run contrary to free enterprise, the heart of the Western economic system.

There is also a danger, as a number of conference participants pointed out, of exaggerating the Soviet need for large inputs of Western technology and capital. The Soviets do not appear to see imports of foreign capital and technology as a substitute for major domestic economic reform or for domestically generated technological achievements. Moreover, they have learned from the experience of some of their allies: Poland, for example, imported large amounts of foreign technology in the 1970s only to find that it lacked the domestic infrastructure, including managerial talent, to utilize it.

Finally, there is the difficulty of getting the West European allies to go along with a strategy linking trade to Soviet domestic reform. This difficulty was underscored by the acrimonious debates within the Western alliance after the Soviet invasion of Afghanistan, the gas-pipeline controversy, and the imposition of martial law in Poland.

A third group, while acknowledging certain risks, points to the opportunities that the changes in the Soviet Union have presented. They argue that the decentralization of decision-making and the diversion of resources to the civilian economy will make it more difficult over the long term for the Soviet Union to embark on a military adventure or a new military spending surge. Second, Gorbachev's new policies are likely to require greater contacts with the West. While admittedly this is no guarantee that the Soviet leadership will pursue a more peaceful course, it does provide opportunities for the West to reduce the Soviet sense of isolation and strengthen the constituencies favoring restraint in Soviet foreign and military policy. Third, Gorbachev's emphasis on joint ventures could open up the Soviet system. Gorbachev has signaled an interest in joining a number of international organizations such as IMF and GATT. At present membership in such organizations seems premature. However, if the Soviet Union should significantly open up its economy, membership might be considered at a later date. Over the long run, this group feels, it is in the West's interest to integrate the Soviet Union more closely into the international economic system.

Regional Issues

The upcoming U.S.-Soviet summit in Washington will concentrate heavily on arms control, especially the signing of an INF agreement. If relations are to be established on a firmer footing, however, the agenda has to be broadened to include other issues, especially the problem of Third World conflicts which might lead to unintentional superpower confrontation. After all, as a number of participants in St. Paul pointed out, it was differences over these issues—Angola, Ethiopia, Afghanistan—which led to the collapse of superpower detente in the mid- and late 1970s. Thus if bilateral relations are to be improved, these issues need to be systematically addressed.

While the U.S. and Soviet views remain far apart on these issues, there have been signs of a shift in Soviet attitudes lately. One sign is a more forthcoming attitude toward the Iran-Iraq war, where superpower interests in avoiding a confrontation and escalation of the conflict to some degree coincide. Another is the shift in the Soviet attitude toward the United Nations and other international organizations. This is reflected in particular in Gorbachev's article printed in *Pravda* on September 17, which a number of conference participants cited. The impact of Gorbachev's statement has been strengthened by his announcement that the Soviet Union will pay its back dues for peace-keeping forces as well as its general dues that have been in arrears. The more forthcoming Soviet attitude could open up new possibilities for strengthening the UN and other multilateral peacekeeping organizations.

One of the first concrete tests of the new Soviet attitude could be in Afghanistan. Indeed, this may be one of the main motivations behind the shift in the Soviet attitude. A UN peacekeeping force might provide an acceptable umbrella for a Soviet withdrawal from Afghanistan. At the same time it would ensure that there would be "no outside interference" by other powers—one of Moscow's chief professed concerns.

The Need for a Domestic Consensus

A final point that emerged from the deliberations in St. Paul is worth mentioning: the need to develop a solid domestic consensus in the United States for America's Soviet policy. What is required is a firm and consistent policy, one that avoids wild oscillations of public mood. This point was underscored by John Whitehead. Too often in the past, he noted, America's perception of the Soviet Union has veered from visions of the millenium to scenes from the apocalypse. This is bad for both countries and also makes our allies nervous.

We share this concern. We believe that there needs to be a more informed debate on United States policy toward the Soviet Union. Both the Task Force Report and the proceedings from the conference in St. Paul are intended to contribute to such a debate. We hope that both endeavors have made a modest but important contribution toward achieving that goal.

John Edwin Mroz
President

F. Stephen Larrabee
Vice President &
Director of Studies

Gorbachev's Stake in the West

by
Bill Bradley
U.S. Senator
(Democrat-New Jersey)

This is a crucial time of change in East-West relations. Opportunity exists to lower tensions and to reduce the risk of confrontation that could lead to nuclear war. The new Gorbachev regime in Moscow talks about "radical reforms" and even a "historic restructuring" of the Soviet system; about "new thinking," "mutual security," a "constructive direction in international relations," and the need to "exclude the possibility of a surprise attack." These are hopefully phrases describing a potentially historic situation in the Soviet Union. But, let's have some perspective.

The USSR in Perspective

Before Mikhail Gorbachev became general secretary, all but the most optimistic Americans would have given low odds to significantly improved relations with the Soviet Union. We saw a nation sinking under the weight of rigid dogmas, economic stagnation, and official corruption, while engaged in a massive military buildup. The Soviet military spanned the globe with a growing navy, a 5-million-person military, and a nuclear force anchored by the biggest, most destructive missiles in the world.

Before Gorbachev, the Soviet leadership seemed paranoid— a history that Europeans and Americans cannot forget:

1939—the Nazi-Soviet pact and the invasion of Finland;

1948—the Berlin blockade;

1953—the armed repression of East Germany;

1956—the invasion of Hungary;

1968—the invasion of Czechoslovakia;

1979—the invasion of Afghanistan;

1981—the imposition of martial law in Poland.

The Cold War gathered momentum when the Soviet Union subverted friendly but independent governments in Eastern Europe. It intensified because of a Western conviction that Stalin's pursuit of security would not stop until all Europe was under his control. Today the division of Europe finds tangible expression in the largest concentration of conventional military power the world has ever seen in peacetime, and it endures because of the differences in political values that are at the core of this conflict.

A society governed by a centralized, one-party state that insists on dictatorial control is inherently unstable. History teaches that instability and greater military power are a dangerous combination. The point is why Soviet power has been such a problem for the rest of the world, especially for Eastern Europe.

Soviet officials have proposed a "new era" before, and we have had previous episodes of summitry and detente.

Remember 1955. The ebullient reformer Nikita Khrushchev is firmly in command and actively engaged in diplomacy toward the West—a diplomacy that included disarmament negotiations, unilateral Soviet troop reduction, and later the famous denunciation of Stalin. The world was eager to believe that the old Cold War was finally thawing and the Soviet military threat to Europe had passed. How rudely these illusions were shattered in 1956 by the Soviet invasion of Hungary.

Salvador de Madariaga, the Spanish Chairman of the Disarmament Commission of the League of Nations, has observed in his memoirs, "Nations don't distrust each other because they're armed; they arm because they distrust each other. And, therefore, to want disarmament before a minimum of common agreement on fundamentals is as absurd as to want people to go undressed in winter. Let the weather be warm and people will discard their clothes readily, and without committees to tell them to undress...."

Prospects for Change

Since Mikhail Gorbachev took office in 1985, we have felt the warm winds of change again; is it too much to hope that the metaphoric warm weather that Madariaga talks about will arrive at last? Can we get more agreement with the Soviets on fundamentals?

General Secretary Gorbachev's emphasis on domestic reform is the single most important new fact in East-West relations. When he became general secretary, annual rates of growth had fallen by more than half in twenty years. Of longer-term industrial and military importance, Soviet high technology lagged far behind the West. General Secretary Gorbachev saw that without the successful implementation of *perestroika*, the Soviet Union would continue to wane as an economic power in the 1990s and, eventually, begin to fade as a military superpower in the twenty-first century.

To maintain its status as a world power at a time of military parity and domestic reform, the Gorbachev leadership proposes a stunning array of diplomatic and arms control proposals—including some positions long advocated by the United States. It says it favors American proposals to cut strategic forces by 50 percent and to ban all intermediate-range nuclear forces. It calls for a nuclear-free Europe, and indeed, the elimination of all nuclear weapons within fifteen years. It revives border talks with China, and discusses withdrawal from Afghanistan. It tries to mediate the Iran-Iraq war at the same time as it calls for better relations with Israel. And in 1988, General Secretary Gorbachev will be the first Soviet leader ever to visit Latin America. All the activity conveys an image of a decisive, flexible Soviet Union—that of a peacemaker and world citizen, worthy of international respect.

So, here we are at the time when the West appears to be weary of the burden of defense, when abhorrence of nuclear weapons is growing, when European parochialism and American isolationism are on the upswing, and when arms control is increasingly perceived as the main means of ensuring NATO's security. Given these facts, how do we respond to this diverse and broad-based challenge from the Soviet Union?

Does Gorbachev's policy offer the West an opportunity? How do we test him to see if constructive change is possible?

It is important to begin at the beginning; we have to know what we want. General Secretary Gorbachev says he wants "mutual security," a "constructive direction in international relations," and a foreign policy "to a greater extent than ever before determined by domestic policy." That's what he wants. What about us? First, we want a more open Soviet society with which we have the possibility for more agreement on fundamentals; one which has faced its past candidly; one which accepts differences in politics, culture, and religion as it shares more power with its people, including minority nationalities. Second, we want greater freedom for Soviet bloc nations, particularly in Eastern Europe, to restructure their own systems. Third, we want more Soviet restraint in the developing world. Fourth, and most of all, we want a lessened prospect of war through a reduction in the conventional offensive military threat against Europe and through a reduction of nuclear arsenals, particularly Soviet counterforce capability.

Many people see the proposed INF treaty to eliminate hundreds of theater nuclear missiles on both sides of the NATO-Warsaw Pact line as the harbinger of a new era in East-West relations.

I, like all of you, hope for a future in which negotiation and mutual agreement to destroy military forces displaces confrontation and the arms race. Like all of you, I hope General Secretary Gorbachev will succeed in finding a new source of authority for the Soviet state—one that doesn't derive from coercive Stalinist campaigns, or a Cold-War view of the outside world as ever menacing and encircling; I hope the general secretary will persuade the Soviet bureaucracy that it no longer makes sense to subordinate the people's desire for a better life to the military's obsession with security; I hope he will convince his elites that Soviet security and prestige depend on sustaining growth and on unleashing popular initiatives. That's what I hope.

But hope is not enough. For the West to be confident that Gorbachev brings the prospect of a new day in East-West relations we will need to see tangible progress in reducing military threats and political repression. We cannot let *perestroika, glasnost'*, and summitry, however encouraging, obscure the fact that issues that have troubled our relationship with the Soviets in the past seem to be unchanged. At the same time we must be flexible enough to seize new opportunities, and to have antennae sensitive enough to hear the soft inner voice of the Soviet Union as well as to pick up the threats.

We need an imaginative yet tough-minded Western strategy. Without a strategy, we will be divided and vulnerable, responding piecemeal, unable to maximize the inherent strength of our alliance. The core of such a strategy must deal seriously with the disparity between weapons inventories and military capabilities of opposing forces in central Europe. It must recognize and use our economic vitality as a strategic asset, and it must see that our ultimate strength lies in what we believe— our values.

The Military Dimension

Let's talk about the military security dimension. About the disparity in conventional forces General Secretary Gorbachev said in mid-September, "If an imbalance or disproportion exists let us remove it." A Western strategy toward the Soviet Union must test this expressed willingness to redress the Soviet imbalance in conventional forces in Europe, as we also reduce our nuclear arsenals.

Everyone has his own view. Mine is the following: based on the best information available the Soviets have built up alarming advantages in their conventional forces over the last two decades. In the mid-1960s, conventional weaponry deployed with active units by NATO and the Warsaw Pact were roughly comparable in the forward areas of central Europe. It would have taken the Soviets months to mobilize enough reserves and reinforcements for a decisive offensive. This ensured clear warning and ample time for NATO to respond effectively.

Since then, the Soviet Union and its partners in the Warsaw Pact have added more than 40,000 tanks, artillery, anti-tank missiles, attack helicopters and other conventional systems. This increase alone is more than all the weapons that NATO had in Europe in 1965. Near NATO's borders the Warsaw Pact has raised its ratio of superiority in tanks to over two-to-one, and in artillery to about three-to-one. It has even gained numerical superiority in anti-tank missile launchers and attack helicopters.

Moreover, Soviet modernization of its weapons in Europe has made them comparable in quality to most of those in the West.

By enlarging its inventories, it also has cut the time required to mobilize an offensive force from months to weeks.

In addition, Soviet military doctrine has reflected this increasingly offensive focus. Not only therefore do Soviet forces outnumber the West in weaponry, but they practice using it in a profoundly threatening way.

Due to these trends—in numbers, quality of weapons, and military doctrine—NATO cannot rely as heavily as before on technological superiority to offset numerical deficiencies in its conventional defenses. Nor can it count on long, clear warning of an offensive buildup on its Eastern borders.

To cope with these problems, NATO relies on a strategy of "flexible response" based on its readiness and ability to use nuclear weapons to resist aggression in Europe. Let's be honest about this problem. As long as the Soviet Union deploys huge offensive conventional forces, especially their modern tank armies, in the center of Europe, the West must preserve the option of a nuclear response.

NATO could minimize this dilemma by building up its conventional defenses. But the economic burdens of strengthening conventional defenses are enormous.

Reducing and reconfiguring Soviet offensive forces in central Europe is the only other way to decrease the risk of a confrontation that could lead to nuclear war. By restructuring Soviet offensive power in Europe the Soviets can demonstrate that they are serious about "mutual security" and a "constructive direction in international relations. " It is also a way for General Secretary Gorbachev to make good on his admonition that "military doctrines must be purely of a defensive nature. " After all, if his emphasis is truly on "domestic policy" in the Soviet Union, how can he see any legitimate need for such potentially menacing forces within a day's drive of Frankfurt, Paris, or Amsterdam?

How do we get the Soviet Union to reduce and reconfigure its forces?

First, let NATO and the Warsaw Pact begin by discussing our respective military doctrines thoroughly and openly before our citizens. Then, let us take some confidence-building measures such as opening up our respective forces—weapons as well as manpower—for mutual scrutiny. And let us count them to establish just what the imbalances and disproportions are. Finally

I would challenge the general secretary to make good on his offer to remove the excess.

Last February General Secretary Gorbachev was prepared to go further—he called for measures to "make it possible to lessen, or better still, altogether exclude the possibility of a surprise attack." The West should immediately follow up this offer with an open mind, searching vigorously for new ways to give ourselves longer and clearer warning of any Soviet mobilization in central Europe. Joint actions worth exploring include monitoring and limiting troop movements, reviewing the status of equipment stockpiles, and providing notification of impending military maneuvers and other exercises.

Asymmetries between the two sides will continue, some of them inherent in the fact that the Soviet Union is so much closer to Germany than the United States and therefore more able to reinforce its forward positions in Europe. Even with these asymmetries, there are actions the Soviet Union could take to contribute to stability: pulling units out of central Europe and simultaneously cutting the total size of its forces in Western Russia and the Ukraine; and giving NATO greater access to information about the readiness of Soviet forces.

Progress on these fronts would make nuclear war even less likely by reducing the risk of any war in Europe. But, as long as NATO is needed to protect freedom in a divided Europe, NATO security will need the ultimate backing of nuclear deterrence.

Lenin said, "Words are deeds. " In a nuclear world, however, on a continent jammed with conventional weapons and competing ideologies, only deeds can exclude the possibility of surprise attack and bring a genuine reduction in tension and a new basis for U.S.-Soviet relations.

The Economic Dimension

That's the security part—but an effective Western strategy must have an economic as well as a military component. The Soviet Union's precarious economic circumstances and Gorbachev's domestic reforms are the source of two new ironies. The first is that Gorbachev cannot accomplish his domestic priorities unless the West is doing well economically. To import technology he must raise cash by borrowing more from the West or by exporting more to the West. Whether he relies on Western capital markets or Western export markets, he will benefit from a healthy Western economy. So, a serious economic downturn could doom Gorbachev's modernization plans. This degree of economic interdependence is new. It challenges the fundamental principle of autarky upon which Soviet security, military success, and political relations with the outside world have been based since the Bolshevik Revolution. It gives the Soviets an unprecedented stake in Western growth.

The second irony stems from the dependence of Gorbachev's reforms on a dramatic increase in domestic investment. He needs to invest in intensive agricultural irrigation; in energy development, especially after Chernobyl; and in machinery, to offset a declining population and to raise labor productivity. And he needs to produce consumer goods that his people can see and want.

The needed investment capital must come either from a reduction in Soviet military spending or from financial markets in the West. He will probably need both. An international environment with less tension could accelerate the reductions in military spending that successful reform will require. There's even an economic rationale. The Soviet Union will be most creditworthy if it frees resources from defense and puts them to work increasing Soviet productivity and improving living standards.

Gorbachev appears to believe that more resources are not enough. There's got to be systemic reform. More resources alone cannot guarantee higher levels of growth. And implementation of his far-reaching program, announced at the June plenum, will be opposed at each step. In the best of circumstances reform will take longer than expected; in the worst of circumstances it will be killed. As opposition grows and pressure builds, access to Western capital will become crucial. That is why the West, while not overstating its importance, should treat its capital as a strategic asset and develop a plan and set of conditions for its flow eastward. Absent such a plan, results could be inconsistent with the West's strategic interest.

As a beginning, let me suggest that the flow of Western capital to the Soviet Union should be limited and proportionate to the progress of systemic reform. Perhaps by bringing the Soviet

Union into the international finance system we would be able to establish some criteria for the provision of loans based on the progress of reform. There could be some basis for denying credit without reform. In present circumstances, there is no discipline, and no accountability for bankers' actions.

In 1985, for example, the Soviet Union owed about $29 billion, including $6 billion of new borrowing. They would like to issue Euronotes, bonds, and other marketable securities. By 1990, their indebtedness is projected to increase substantially with most of the new money coming from West European and Japanese banks. The Soviets reportedly get these loans on very favorable terms, even from U.S. banking institutions. Earlier this year, a major American bank announced it was the lead bank in a $300-million loan to the Soviet Union at a mere one-eighth of a percent over LIBOR, the international lending rate. Meanwhile, a new democracy in Latin America, such as Brazil, has to pay 2¼ percent above LIBOR.

The banking community argues these rates reflect risk, that it's sound commercial practice to lend cheap to the Soviets and dear to Latin American democracies. The Soviets, it is said, are likely to repay on time—just like Chile's authoritarian government. That might be true now. But to lend without awareness of the strategic consequences and without alliance conditionality is shortsighted. If we make reform a vigorous criterion for lending, we then encourage General Secretary Gorbachev to push ahead on his present course. Probably it's worth a try.

At the very least, we need to recognize that General Secretary Gorbachev's expressed objectives, and his strategy to attain them, present us with a unique opportunity. Without Western capital and technology, the Soviets can increase domestic investment only by decreasing military spending. I question the wisdom—and the morality—of helping the Soviets avoid the choice between civilian investment and military buildups, especially while we force harsher decisions on struggling democracies where people are starving. Surely, if we demand economic reform as a condition for interest rate relief or new loans in the Third World, it would seem only prudent to insist on similarly stringent reform criteria before permitting the Soviet Union to borrow on more favorable terms.

Reallocating scarce resources away from the conventional

forces massed in central Europe wouldn't be a bad place for them to start. The West is under enormous pressure from our own electorates to cut defense spending; part of that comes from the economic pain of budget deficits caused by expensive defense programs. It would be striking indeed to hold the Soviets to a lesser standard or to help them cope with their economic problems by bailing them out of the pressures on their military budget.

The Political and Ideological Dimension

So we need a military component and an economic component. Finally, in addition to economic and military components a Western strategy must include a political and ideological component as well. We must never shy away from comparing the Soviet Union and the West in terms of freedom and quality of life. We must be proud that we value not just the freedom of our nation but the liberty of each individual man and woman. Western democratic culture derives from the Enlightenment belief that freedom is a universal aspiration and the essence of man. It should not be bargained or yielded at any price.

We should never hesitate to point out the Soviet Union's shortcomings on human rights, for they will never hesitate to point out our shortcomings. But at the same time we have to be attuned to the possibility of change even in the Soviet Union. We will watch and applaud if the Soviets go beyond *glasnost'*, which is only permission to speak, and establish freedom of speech which is guaranteed under law. We will praise a Soviet Union in which people have a bigger voice in what the economy produces. We will cheer a Soviet Union that confronts its past and allows its people to emigrate and its families to reunite. Such a Soviet Union would be a safer neighbor for Europe and less of a threat to the United States.

Conclusion

Exploiting opportunities and providing incentives to move European security and U.S.-Soviet relations to a new ground will be one of the most important challenges for the next administration, whether Democratic or Republican. U.S.

leadership should emphasize a combination of an unyielding adherence to the ideals of political liberty and a receptivity to political reform in the Soviet Union. We are at the beginning of a process that may hold great promise. But to realize that promise, we must plan our approach carefully—not as a unilateral American exercise but in genuine consultation with our allies. The challenge and opportunity of the next few years is not just to improve U.S.-Soviet relations. It is to work with our allies and with the Soviets to build a new security framework for Europe and the world and to achieve what has eluded us for so long—a lasting peace.

Towards a Strategy for Progress

by
Hans-Dietrich Genscher
Minister for Foreign Affairs of the Federal Republic of Germany

This meeting of ours is taking place at a time of important developments and decisions. It occurs at one of those moments when, as one of my fellow participants in this meeting, Senator Bradley, put it, "a door long closed may be opening to show us the path to new places, new vistas of hope and progress for the human race." As always during such phases of development, opportunities and risks lie side by side. It is up to us to help determine the course to be followed by man—whether he will pursue the path towards a better future or whether he will drift towards the abyss of self-destruction. No generation before us has had to bear such great responsibility as we do. Technological developments offer us the key to a more humane world. However, if we fail to meet our responsibilities, we also have the capacity to destroy ourselves.

A Community in Quest of Survival

A Chinese proverb says, "May you live in interesting times." Whether we like it not, we are living in interesting times. The structures of international politics and the world economy are in a state of flux. Fundamental changes are occurring in relations between West and East, in the North-South relationship, in the world economy and in the ecological field. These changes are closely interconnected and interactive. International politics are no longer determined solely by relations between Washington and Moscow; new centers of power are emerging. The People's Republic of China is one of them. The European Community is taking its place in international politics. It does so as a partner, an ally and a friend of the United States. Regional groupings are emerging in various parts of the world, such as ASEAN and the Gulf Cooperation Council. India and Japan are becoming more influential. The nonaligned movement is emerging as a factor of stability in the Third World.

At the same time, the world population has passed the 5-billion mark. The debt crisis weighs heavily on the world economy. It threatens the economic, social and political future of many heavily indebted countries. It also poses a serious threat to the creditor countries and jeopardizes the common will of North and South to cooperate with each other. The chasm between overproduction of raw materials in the developing countries and the leveling or even stagnating demand for raw materials in the industrialized countries continues to widen. We must help the developing countries to process their raw materials into finished goods or intermediate products. Whoever seeks to restrict the developing countries to the role of raw material and energy suppliers to the world market is depriving them of any prospects for the future.

A new technological revolution is taking place. Information technology, biotechnology, materials technology, renewable-energy technology and space technology are leading mankind into a new age. The chances of overcoming diseases and epidemics are improving. The new forms of technology enable us to adopt environmentally safe production processes; they offer us effective methods of healing our environment. Resolution of the conflict between economic growth and environmental protection is becoming possible. The new forms of technology are also leading us away from the age of the masses; they can take us to a new stage in the development of freedom. They are leading towards a society marked by a new individuality, self-reliance and creativity. Their trademarks are decentralization and the dismantling of hierarchical structures, as well as the development of individual lifestyles and human personality.

However, no less great than the opportunities of the future are the dangers of the present. The entire human race is living in one cohesive ecological system. The abuse of vital natural resources in one country has repercussions on all others, even in far-off regions of the world. For thousands of years, nature seemed to be inexhaustible and indestructible. Modern technology, however, could upset the ecological balance. The world climate is being impaired. The ozone layer, which protects us against hazardous radiation from outer space, is being damaged. At the same time, the power of modern weapons of mass destruction is threatening all life on earth. In the nuclear age there will be no postwar period. We must create a new global code of ethics, which proclaims the effects of technology on nature to be part of the responsibility of mankind. We must recognize our duty to future generations.

Today's intriguing developments, revealing to us new horizons and new dangers, call for new responsibility and new answers. By "us" I mean the entire human race in West and East, in North and South. Almost without noticing, we have become a community in quest of survival. Responsible foreign policy must be perceived as global domestic policy.

New Challenges

In the Soviet Union, new leaders are calling for new thinking and reforms in order to solve the country's internal problems. They are calling for a reshaping of foreign relations and are constantly astounding the world with new arms control and disarmament proposals. In view of these developments, the West needs a comprehensive political and economic strategy which will enable it to live up to its responsibility.

I want to focus on how we can shape relations between West and East. In the past, it was pressure and threats generated by the Soviet Union which made the West close ranks time and again. This impetus provided for the establishment of NATO, for the strengthening of Euro-American relations and for progress in the unification of the European democracies. The Korean crisis, the Berlin ultimatum and the Soviet SS-20 buildup are examples.

Today we face a different challenge—the challenge that derives from the new thinking and behavior of the new Soviet leaders, the challenge to improve relations between West and East and hence to seize new opportunities for mankind when they present themselves. Is that not an equally powerful stimulus for Western solidarity, for Western vigor, for a Western strategy in pursuit of a better world? We must fit our Western community for the future. We must make it even more of an alliance for progress. At times of dramatic developments in East-West relations, we cannot afford stagnation within the Western community. Western policy must not lose its equilibrium. We want to have positive dynamism in relations between West and East, but we need at least the same dynamism in the development of the Western community.

That also means creating at long last the European pillar of the NATO alliance. Europe can satisfy its claim to equal partnership with the United States in formulating overall Western policy within the alliance only if it makes its influence felt as a cohesive unit. Our will to unite Europe economically, politically, and in the security field consolidates and strengthens the alliance. America, too, needs a Europe which responsibly and confidently takes its place in the alliance and in international politics. That requires the development of the European Community into a European Union, including the integration of Western Europe in the field of security. France and Germany have a key role to play in this process. The revitalization of the Western European Union is intended to build the European pillar of NATO; its aim is not to create a sort of alternative NATO.

Relations between Europe and America are also faced with challenges in the fields of economic, monetary, and trade policy. At a time when the West is called upon to be active in taking advantage of the opportunities offered by the East-West relationship, it must not dissipate its energies in a trade conflict between Europe and America. Every step towards the elimination of protectionism has strengthened the West and enhanced its prospects for the future; every relapse into protectionism will weaken it. Particularly at the present time, when relations between West and East are moving forward and new vistas are opening up, we need the closest possible coordination between Europe and the United States in all areas.

Our policy towards the East must proceed from a basic appreciation of the fact that none of the major problems in today's world can be solved if East and West continue to waste their political energies and economic potential on confrontation and the arms race. At the same time, we are aware that the West and the East possess radically different systems with fundamentally different values and structures. Nevertheless, confrontation between industrialized countries of the North is an anachronism which can no longer be tolerated by a world that has grown into a community in quest of survival. Its elimination has become a basic prerequisite of human survival and of a better future for mankind. Mr. Gorbachev has expressed this in similar words: "Our world," he has said, "is united not only through the internationalization of economic life and through the potent information and communication media, but also through the common danger of nuclear extermination, ecological disaster and a global explosion of the tension between poverty and affluence."

Western Choices

On the first of February this year, I spoke in Davos, Switzerland, on the theme "Let us take Mr. Gorbachev seriously; let us hold him to his word." Subsequent developments have endorsed the analysis and cautious prediction undertaken in that speech, in which I highlighted the opportunities as well as the limitations of a new policy. I defined Mr. Gorbachev's intentions as follows: "It is not a question of introducing Western-style democracy but of creating more possibilities for individual development within the framework of the existing system." There can be no doubt that the system in the Soviet Union is a socialist one and that Mr. Gorbachev intends it to remain so. The policy of reform is meant to make Soviet society more efficient but not to challenge the system as such. Anyone who expected anything else is either a victim of wishful thinking or has not read Mr. Gorbachev's speeches.

The West has to decide whether to adopt a "wait-and-see" attitude to developments in the Soviet Union or whether to set about examining how they can be used for the establishment of a new and constructive relationship between West and East. If the internal development in the Soviet Union improves that country's ability to engage in the broadest possible cooperation with the West, the West for its part must encourage such development through its actions and reactions. In a world dependent on cooperation, this is also in the interests of the West. Here, too, interdependence prevails.

In the West, people are asking whether the Soviet Union merely seeks to win breathing space. This theory is refuted by the fact that *glasnost'* and, even more so, *perestroika,* the reshaping of the economy and society, are processes which will take many years, probably even decades. By then, however, the world, and the

Soviet Union within that world, will have altered to such an extent that it is almost impossible to imagine Moscow returning to its policy of the pre-Gorbachev era as if nothing had happened.

People are also asking whether such a policy of reform can be carried out at all in the Soviet Union. Mr. Gorbachev will be aware of the difficulties, perhaps even more so now than when he first took office. The main problem may well be that successes can only very gradually become apparent to the people of the Soviet Union. A great deal of patience will be required. But Mr. Gorbachev has recognized that the Soviet Union simply cannot continue as before without destroying its own prospects for the future. The concentration of the country's energies on armaments and the expansionist foreign policy of the pre-Gorbachev period overtaxed the Soviet economy and society. It also mobilized the resistance of the West.

Mr. Gorbachev inherited a difficult legacy. Bureaucratization, unwillingness to take responsibility and a lack of creativity, as well as widespread popular apathy, were stifling economic development. The technological gap between the Soviet Union and the West was growing ever wider. The People's Republic of China, which was prepared to make reforms, was opening itself to the West. That was the situation when Mikhail Gorbachev took office as general secretary in March 1985. And this is the very real background to the new thinking.

Mr. Gorbachev is trying to effect a fundamental change of course. He wants to make economic growth and technological progress the paramount goals of his policy. These goals, however, cannot be approached in isolation; they cannot be achieved solely through economic reform. Mr. Gorbachev also needs people who are motivated to achieve, who think independently and who are prepared to accept responsibility. In other words, he must launch a reform of society.

Indeed, he must reform the entire policy of the Soviet Union. He himself speaks of truly revolutionary tasks. This purpose is served by *glasnost'*, which means greater openness—in the media, too—in discussing the problems inherent in the system, though it does not imply questioning the system itself. The same purpose is served by *perestroika*. This does not, I repeat, mean democracy in the Western sense. But it is intended to inject dynamism into Soviet society. A greater measure of legal consistency is to be created, although we should not expect the adoption of the rule of law as we know it in the West. The power and unwieldiness of the huge bureaucracies, which stifle any creativity, are to be curbed. In his Murmansk speech [October 1], Mr. Gorbachev called for drastic cuts in the number of people employed in public administration.

In order to overcome the backwardness of the economy, Mr. Gorbachev also needs a new foreign policy, a policy which creates stability in external relations. The cost of an expansionist foreign policy is to be reduced, the arms burden lightened, and economic, technological, and financial cooperation with the West developed. Detente and cooperation in relations with the West are of central importance to the success of Mr. Gorbachev's internal reform policy. That is why he says that coexistence is not only the absence of war but a way of living together for states with differing political systems, a way which allows for mutually beneficial cooperation and mutual assistance in the solution of global problems. Security, he says, is not only a military but also a political responsibility. The security of one side cannot be achieved at the other side's expense; joint security is necessary.

The offer made by the West is expressed in the aim formulated in NATO's Harmel Report back in 1967: "...to achieve a just and lasting peaceful order in Europe accompanied by appropriate security guarantees." Since 1975, we have had the CSCE Final Act as a comprehensive guide to the construction of such a peaceful order in Europe. Today we can say in retrospect that the path taken in the Helsinki Final Act was and remains the right one. Both German states, the Federal Republic of Germany and the German Democratic Republic, through the way they shape their relations, render considerable contributions within the framework of the CSCE process to the improvement of the situation in Europe.

The CSCE process withstood the serious strains experienced during the first half of the 1980s. Today, under new favorable conditions, we must do all we can to promote it. We seek progress in the three main areas of the Final Act, namely

- in the establishment of stable security;

- in the intensification of cooperation in all areas; and

- in the realization of human rights.

Let me deal first with security. The Reykjavik summit meeting between President Reagan and General Secretary Gorbachev in October 1986 brought about, as we can now say with confidence, the breakthrough to genuine disarmament. This meeting saw the establishment of new thinking on the future of relations between West and East and on disarmament, thinking marked by awareness of responsibility for the survival of mankind. The INF agreement will be a first step along this path. It will bring the complete and worldwide elimination of all land-based intermediate-range forces. An entire category of weapons will thereby be abolished once and for all. That is a success unprecedented in the history of disarmament and it is a success for the alliance, as well as a personal success for my friend George Shultz.

My government contributed substantially to the agreement in principle on the INF accord. It is therefore wrong to assert that the INF agreement undermines Europeans' confidence in the United States. The opposite is true. From the very beginning, since the adoption of the NATO double-track decision of December 1979, the zero option has been the proposal of the Western alliance. The fact that the Soviet Union has now accepted this proposal confirms that resolve, combined with a constructive approach, pays dividends. How can it be damaging to the West to achieve its disarmament objective after years of negotiations?

It is also wrong to see in the INF agreement the danger of Europe becoming decoupled from the United States. On the contrary, this agreement is emphatically welcomed by the vast majority of the public in the Federal Republic of Germany and in Europe. That increases the cohesion of our transatlantic partnership. In the 1970s, the Soviet SS-20 buildup was rightly described as an attempt to decouple Europe's security from that of the United States. How, then, can the elimination of the Soviet SS-20 threat likewise lead to decoupling?

What must now be done is to extend the disarmament effort to cover the entire arms spectrum. For this purpose, the alliance possesses a comprehensive and coherent disarmament strategy, which was endorsed by the ministerial meeting of the North Atlantic Council at Reykjavik in 1987. The agreement in principle on intermediate-range missiles is, after all, only a first step. A process has been set in motion which must be made irreversible. It must lead to a comprehensive and stable disarmament regime. We firmly support the intention of the United States administration to reach agreement with the Soviet Union on drastic reductions of strategic offensive weapons. We are convinced that the Soviet Union has the same objective. As we decided at the North Atlantic Council meeting, we shall expedite NATO preparations for the negotiations on nuclear missiles with a range below 500 kilometers. In this area Eastern superiority is particularly marked; because of our geographical situation, we Germans are acutely aware of our exposure to the threat from these weapons.

We regard as particularly urgent the conclusion of the negotiations on the worldwide prohibition of chemical weapons. An ever-increasing number of the world's nations, including Third World countries, are arming themselves with chemical weapons. During the 1960s we checked the danger of the proliferation of nuclear weapons by means of the Non-Proliferation Treaty. Today we must avert once and for all the danger of chemical-weapons proliferation by banning such weapons worldwide. Chemical weapons must not become a nuclear-weapons substitute for the nuclear have-nots.

Progress in nuclear disarmament makes the establishment of conventional stability in Europe all the more important. We seek to establish this stability at a low level of weapons by means of disarmament. No state should be capable of attacking; each should be able only to defend. The strategy proposed by the West for this purpose will strengthen security in every single part of Europe. In view of the Soviet Union's conventional superiority, we regard the Soviet willingness to consider asymmetrical reductions as an important step forward. It is time to draw up the blueprint for a peaceful order in Europe. That requires more than just disarmament.

To prevent any kind of war in Europe forever and to secure lasting peace; to gain more stability through political dialogue and cooperation in all fields; to bring people closer together again in divided Europe, and hence in divided Germany, too, by means of unhindered contacts and free exchanges of opinion and information; to implement human rights—these aims are the core of the political philosophy underlying the Helsinki Final Act.

Economic Cooperation

Extensive economic cooperation can also contribute to the

achievement of these goals. In the economic field, international interdependence is growing. The development of the new forms of advanced technology is so exacting and costly that it requires international cooperation between companies, as well as worldwide markets. One single global market is emerging. In this development the states of COMECON remain on the sidelines. Their trade with the Western industrialized countries and with the developing countries remains at a very low level. For the Federal Republic of Germany, the Soviet Union's principal Western trading partner, transactions with the Soviet Union amount to barely 2 percent of our external trade. To Switzerland alone we export three times as much as to the Soviet Union. The situation is no different with regard to industrial cooperation and international direct investment, the fastest-growing areas of the world economy today, in which the East takes virtually no part. The Soviet leaders are aware that, if this isolation continues, the Soviet Union has no chance of catching up with world economic and technological development. It has evidently been recognized in Moscow, too, that entry into the information age alters societies and indeed demands openness and exchanges. No country in the world, regardless of size, can shut itself off from this development; if it does, the price it pays is national recession and detachment from worldwide progress.

Closer integration of the Soviet Union and COMECON into the world economy is also in our Western interest. More intensive economic relations between West and East promote stability and confidence. An increase in economic exchanges ultimately means accepting mutual dependence. That, however, creates interest in improving the entire spectrum of relations between West and East. Furthermore, the need to become internationally competitive forces structural adjustments, thereby supporting the process of reform in the Soviet Union.

In the West, people ask whether the Soviet Union might not become stronger as a result of economic cooperation. Of course, economic cooperation can take place only if it benefits both sides. The question is this: Does economic cooperation make the Soviet Union on the whole more predictable and more able to cooperate? And we must also decide whether enormous differences in economic performance and in people's living standards tend to increase or decrease tension. Those differences in productivity and living standards which have their roots in the socialist system cannot be eliminated by us; that has to be done by the Soviet leadership. And this is precisely the aim of the modernization campaign. The question of how far this aim will be achievable within the bounds of the system must be answered in Moscow. But in an interdependent world it is in our own interests not to heighten these destabilizing differences by refusing to cooperate. We must not compound the political and ideological division with economic and technological divisions.

Soviet Initiatives

Since Mr. Gorbachev took office two and a half years ago, we have most certainly observed changes in Soviet foreign and security policy. The Soviet leaders have overcome the immobility which marked Soviet foreign policy in recent years. They are evidently trying to take an active part in shaping East-West relations by means of new initiatives. Of importance to arms control and disarmament is the willingness of the Soviet Union to agree to inspections, including challenge on-site inspections. This makes verification possible. There are indications that the Soviet Union is rethinking its position within the world economy and redefining this position—although that will certainly be a long process. Greater scope is being given for internal development in the other socialist states of the Soviet power bloc. These more encouraging signals contrast, however, with unfulfilled expectations, particularly the failure to end the war in Afghanistan. In this context, words must at last be followed by deeds.

A Soviet Union which seeks a comprehensive and lasting improvement in East-West relations will find the West to be a constructive and responsible partner. The Western attitude must depend on our interests concerning the development we desire. If today, after decades of East-West confrontation, a turning point is attainable, it would be a mistake of historic dimensions if the West were to miss this opportunity. We look soberly at the facts, but we will not allow ourselves to be shackled by outdated thinking and deep-seated antipathies. Whoever takes the worst-case scenario as the sole basis of his action, including his action vis-à-vis the Soviet Union, becomes a political deadweight.

We are convinced of the vitality of our liberal order and of the capability of our Western alliance to defend itself. For this reason, we will not let timidity or a lack of self-assurance make us doubt Mr. Gorbachev's intention to implement domestic and foreign policy reforms; we take these intentions seriously, and we are just as seriously prepared to engage in cooperation. Part of disarmament is the elimination of ingrained antipathy—on both sides.

The internal development in the Soviet Union is, after all, not just a domestic occurrence with no impact on the outside world. A Soviet Union which is adopting more open domestic and foreign policies is a better partner, above all a more predictable partner, for the West than a Soviet Union which seals itself off from the outside world and becomes increasingly hidebound in its internal affairs. The greater openness of the Soviet Union at home and abroad strengthens its capacity for cooperation.

Building Security

Our Western position is unequivocal—we do not wish to compel the other side to arm itself to death, nor do we wish to force anyone to his knees by economic means. We wish to build confidence through cooperation. We wish to serve the cause of common survival and the interests of all mankind. We must create dependence in the best sense of the word, dependence which will make peace and cooperation irreversible. Our political approach must enable us both to guarantee our security wherever it is threatened and to pursue a constructive policy towards the East wherever there is an opportunity to do so.

This approach is reflected in the twofold strategy outlined by the Harmel Report, which the alliance adopted in 1967. Today, as West and East make a fresh start towards mutual understanding, this approach is more relevant than ever. The point is that NATO has never restricted itself to securing peace with military means alone. We also seek to secure peace politically on the basis of a coordinated overall strategy. A security policy based only on autonomous military efforts could no longer begin to guarantee security in a nuclear world. Cooperation and cooperative security structures between West and East are called for.

It would be wrong to restrict our policy towards the East to disarmament negotiations. The political dialogue and cooperation between West and East in business, science, technology and environmental protection must lead to ever more joint action for the future of mankind. That helps to create confidence.

Crucial to further progress in the CSCE process and to the development of trust, cooperation and detente between West and East is respect for human rights. The CSCE Final Act enshrined respect for human rights as one of its fundamental principles. In the words of that document, respect for human rights is "an essential factor" for "peace, justice and well-being." That must become reality. If 3 million of the 17 million Germans in the German Democratic Republic have received permission from their authorities this year to visit us in the Federal Republic of Germany, that is a great step forward for these people. If an amnesty is proclaimed which includes political prisoners, that is a step forward, too. If thousands of Soviet citizens of German and Jewish extraction are now allowed to leave the Soviet Union forever, this means that freedom of movement is being implemented for thousands of people.

But there is still a lot of work to be done, much of it elementary. Many of the pledges made in the Helsinki Final Act have yet to be honored. The release of Andrei Sakharov must be followed by the release of the many lesser-known people in similar situations. The famous names must not blind us to the many unknown persons. The value of any policy is measurable by its effect on individuals.

The new challenges to mankind confront both West and East, but they require a greater change in thought and action from the East than from the West. Our open Western societies have a greater propensity for change than the bureaucratic socialist systems with their doctrinaire ideologies. Why, one must ask, should our democracies, based on freedom and human dignity, shun the competition between the systems? The more we fulfill our own ideals, the more liberal our systems, the better shall we be armed for this competition. And we demand no more from the communist states than what they undertook to fulfill in the Helsinki Final Act.

Nothing can obscure the fact that in a world full of weapons of mass destruction, in a world of new technological opportunities and dangers, there can only be honest and serious efforts to foster cooperation. I belong to a nation which is divided into two states, just as Europe is divided. The competition between the systems takes place where we live, where two systems of values confront each other, where two highly armed alliances face each other; there we find the greatest concentration of nuclear and conventional weapons and forces; environmental problems accumulate because of our position at the heart of a continent, because of our population density and our high degree of industrialization.

With this in mind, we fulfill our commitments in the Western alliance. We bear the brunt of responsibility for the conventional defense of Europe. We shall never forget that 300,000 American servicemen and their families stand by us in this task. We know that freedom has it price, that it is not given to us. History has taught us Germans our lesson. That was expressed for all Germans by the President of the Federal Republic of Germany, Richard von Weizsäcker, in his memorable speech on May 8, 1985.

The place of the Federal Republic of Germany is on the side of freedom; we belong to the community of Western democracies. We are not drifters between two worlds. The path to neutralism would be the path to self-isolation for us. It would make us a pawn of other countries' interests and an object of rivalry between West and East. That is another reason why we are such staunch advocates of Western unity. But we also know that West and East have the choice of perishing in confrontation or surviving in cooperation.

I therefore stand by my appeal—let us take Mr. Gorbachev seriously; let us hold him to his word. Let us try to bring about a new order of East-West relations together with the new Soviet leaders. Let us intensify our cooperation. Let us protect our vital natural resources for ourselves and for all future generations. Let us take bold steps towards disarmament. We shall only be successful in this effort, we shall only attain more security and more stability, if our Western community acts together.

We must let our every decision be guided by our fundamental values—freedom and human dignity, civil and social rights and the right of all peoples to self-determination. But freedom and human dignity exist only where there is life. Human rights and the right to self-determination will only continue to obtain if mankind survives.

That is the message of the Western democracies—a world of human dignity, social justice, peace, and freedom. That is the strategy for progress, for which we seek universal acceptance. To this end, we want to go on developing our Western community; to this end, we seek cooperation with the East.

The Necessity of New Thinking for International Relations in Our Nuclear and Space Age:
The GDR's Policy of Dialogue and Understanding

by
Harry Ott
Deputy Minister of Foreign Affairs and
Permanent Representative of the
German Democratic Republic to the United Nations

At the very outset, I should like to thank the President of the Institute for East-West Security Studies, Mr. John Edwin Mroz, and the distinguished members of the Board of Directors of the Institute for the kind invitation and the opportunity to speak before this august forum of prominent politicians, scientists, journalists, and representatives of the business world about several aspects of the foreign policy of the German Democratic Republic. This conference testifies to the growing interest in this country in the policy of the Soviet Union and other socialist states, including that of my own country.

In a few weeks from now, the seventieth anniversary of the Great October Socialist Revolution will be commemorated all over the world. Today there can hardly be any doubt that the Russian Revolution has become the most important event of this century and has challenged mankind to a rethinking—that is, to new thinking. For the first time in history peace and cooperation between peoples were decreed as the supreme doctrine of the state and war was declared illegal. An entirely new type of state and social system came into existence and turned out to be a challenge to the entire world.

Today's policy of new thinking, of *perestroika* and *glasnost'* in the Soviet Union, also constitutes a challenge, although in other dimensions. New thinking in our nuclear and space age, demonstrated by far-reaching Soviet peace proposals, is an appeal to common sense and realism. My country and people welcome and support the policy adopted at the 27th Congress of the Communist Party of the Soviet Union because it serves peace and the well-being of man and promotes security, confidence, and cooperation.

The policy pursued by General Secretary Gorbachev is serious and honest, it leaves no room for speculations, allegations or any illusions. Would not the best litmus test for new thinking be taking up General Secretary Gorbachev's proposals and initiatives and taking him "by his word"? New thinking is not a present from General Secretary Gorbachev, nor does it imply a need to give him gifts. Rather, it is the dictate of the hour and mutually beneficial. It is an appeal to all states and peoples— large or small, whether in the East or West, South or North— to recognize and bear their common responsibility for the destiny of mankind and to act accordingly. It is in this spirit that we participate in this conference and take the floor.

For the first time in its history mankind is capable of solving many problems that have so far hindered its progress. Through qualitative changes of the material basis of our life, through the scientific and technological revolution, the potential has arisen for ensuring a decent life for all people on our planet for the last quarter of this century.

At the same time, dangers have emerged which put into question the further existence of mankind. Nuclear weapons in connection with high technology have given rise to an entirely new situation, the denial of which would have fatal consequences. Therefore, the question of new thinking is today directly related to the question of life. There is only one alternative, namely to survive together or perish together. This is the cardinal question of international policy; it is the "categorical imperative," as our great German philosopher Immanuel Kant would have formulated it.

It is also the starting point for our call for new thinking in our time. May I recall Albert Einstein and Bertrand Russell stated in 1955 out of humanist responsibility and scientific vision regarding the existence of nuclear weapons: "We must learn to think in a new way. Instead of asking which steps can be taken to ensure victory for the system we prefer—because such steps no longer exist—we have to ask the question which steps can be taken to prevent a military conflict whose consequences would be disastrous for all sides."

New political thinking and action in our nuclear and space age, in my view, is comprised of the following:

- Today, peace can no longer be achieved by arming against each other. More weapons bring less security. Even large military potentials no longer guarantee greater security.

- Nuclear weapons are unusable, as will be other weapons with increasingly destructive capabilities. Their use would lead to self-annihilation.

- The danger of war can only be removed by political means— by the limitation and final liquidation of stockpiled weapons.

- It becomes ever more evident that the security of states, traditionally defined as national security, can no longer be reached adversarially. National security can only be ensured through mutual cooperation at the international level, that is, beyond the boundaries of political systems.

- Mankind is faced with a great number of other global problems which require urgent, joint solutions. There is a growing interdependence of political, military, economic, ecological, humanitarian and other questions. Thus, all states—large, medium, and small—whether they are aware of it or not, bear a global responsibility for solving those problems.

The aim of new political thinking and action can, therefore, only be a stable and durable order of peace in a world that excludes war—whether nuclear or conventional—as a means of policy; that peacefully settles conflicts between states on the basis of agreed procedures; and that recognizes and respects every people's right to self-determination.

A Breakthrough in Ideas

New thinking—that means a breakthrough of the idea of comprehensive security.

One year ago, the proposal for establishing a comprehensive system of international peace and security was submitted at the United Nations. After a broad and open discussion, the contours of that concept can now be seen. There are four main pillars supporting the concept, namely political-military, economic, ecological, and humanitarian aspects. Its implementation could be reached within the framework of the United Nations, and through the United Nations on the basis of its Charter.

Security in the political-military field does not only mean, in our view, recognition of the fact that nuclear war cannot be won and must never be fought. Security means, above all, taking concrete measures for a step-by-step elimination of nuclear weapons and all other weapons of mass destruction. Great importance must be attached, in this context, to the accord of the Soviet Union and the United States to agree, in principle, to the global elimination of their land-based intermediate-range and short-range missiles. Such an agreement and its practical implementation without ifs and buts would indeed be the materialized expression of new thinking and the start of nuclear disarmament proper. At the same time, such an agreement would favor progress in other fields, for instance in the negotiations on the 50-percent reduction of strategic offensive weapons under strict observance of the ABM Treaty. This historic chance must be used. We sincerely wish that our children and grandchildren will be able to say, and that it will be written in golden letters in the annals of history, that the turnaround to peace, disarmament and security was brought about in the fall of 1987, that President Ronald Reagan and General Secretary Mikhail Gorbachev had the vision and the courage—despite all differences in policies and ideologies—to give priority to the questions determining the destiny of mankind.

May I also recall that the states party to the Warsaw Treaty at their Berlin summit last May proposed a complex program of concrete disarmament steps. No kind of weapon is left out of that proposal, and it foresees the strictest measures of control and verification. This establishes an alternative to the strategy of "nuclear deterrence." The allied socialist states declare in their exclusively defensive military doctrine that they will never under any circumstances initiate military action against any state or alliance of states unless they are themselves the target of an armed attack; that they will never be the first to employ nuclear weapons; that they have no territorial claims on any other state, either in Europe or outside Europe; and that they do not view any state or any people as their enemy.

Military imbalances that have emerged regarding any kind of weapon must be reduced through disarmament by the side that has the advantage over the other, in order to restore the balance at a lower level.

Why, we ask, should it not be possible to have direct negotiations between NATO and the Warsaw Treaty, to reach an agreement on a "strategy of defense"?

The German Democratic Republic has a fundamental interest in and a specific responsibility for reducing military confrontation and replacing it with understanding and cooperation. We want to establish peace with ever fewer weapons, we want to proceed from one zero solution to the other. No kind of weapon is left out by us. Our intention is to facilitate global solutions with the help of regional steps. Therefore we have made initiatives to establish a nuclear-weapons-free corridor and a chemical-weapons-free zone in central Europe, given sustained support to the Jaruzelski Plan for thinning out armed forces and armaments in central Europe, and made committed efforts toward implementing the agreements reached in the CSCE process, in particular under the Stockholm Document. We express the hope that the Vienna CSCE follow-up conference will be concluded with a balanced and substantive result, in particular with a mandate for a negotiation forum on disarmament in the conventional field.

Security in the economic field means full implementation of the principles of equality, mutual advantage, and non-discrimination in international economic relations. It means seeking joint solutions to urgent problems existing in the world economy while taking into account the legitimate interests of all sides. This refers to settling the problems of foreign indebtedness and overcoming underdevelopment, as well as eliminating illegal boycott measures and the policy of embargo. The German Democratic Republic believes that the extension of economic, scientific, and technological relations creates a stable material basis for the process of detente and strengthens predictability and trust in intergovernmental relations.

As is well known, environmental pollution does not stop at

national frontiers. To a growing extent, all states are involved in questions of ecological security. Convincing proof of that has been furnished by the substantive report of the Brundtland Commission, *Our Common Future,* which has received a positive response. The necessity of purposeful, coordinated international cooperation in the ecological field becomes ever more urgent. As an industrialized country situated in the very heart of Europe, the German Democratic Republic has a special interest in solving environmental problems and contributes its internationally recognized share to that end. International cooperation is also required for solving other global problems, such as, for instance, combating AIDS or drug and alcohol abuse.

Security in the humanitarian field means a broad promotion of cooperation especially in the field of human rights. The idea of comprehensive security is, therefore, directed at implementing the most fundamental human tasks, namely to prevent war and to guarantee the supreme human right, the right to live in peace. The socioeconomic foundations for the free development of the people have been laid in the German Democratic Republic. Social security, full employment, social justice, and opportunities for education for all—as they exist in my country—are a *sine qua non* for democracy and the enjoyment of all human rights. Political, civil, economic, social, and cultural rights are being implemented in their entirety. This also includes, of course, keeping the people informed—which is fully ensured in the German Democratic Republic.

Foreign Policy Responsibilities

The GDR is especially committed to the philosophy of new thinking. Our commitment stems from the historical responsibility and the bitter experience of two world wars that originated from German soil. It is also due to the geographical situation of my country, at the dividing line between the two most powerful military alliances and in a region with the highest concentration of nuclear and conventional destructive potential. It explains the efforts of the German Democratic Republic to do everything to ensure, in accordance with its Constitution, that war will never again emanate from German soil. Through a results-oriented political dialogue we wish to contribute our share so that common sense and realism prevail in international relations.

The German Democratic Republic ranks, as you know, among the leading industrialized countries in the world. It is a country where for one and a half decades now a large-scale sociopolitical program is being implemented for all people; a country where culture and science, the health and educational systems and, of course, the field of sports have reached a very high level. Its international relations are based on its alliance with the Soviet Union and the other socialist states. We maintain close and friendly relations with Asian, African and Latin American states. The policy of dialogue, understanding, and cooperation with Western states that has been pursued for many years by the GDR aims to focus on common, overarching questions and to develop mutually advantageous relations between states; to use every possible opportunity for discussions, talks, and consultations; and to work consistently toward finding solutions to disputed questions wherever they exist or emerge.

New political thinking entails a qualitatively higher level of foreign-policy responsibilities. Peace begins on one's own doorstep. What was possible and needed in this respect was illustrated by the recent official visit of our head of state, Erich Honecker, to the Federal Republic of Germany. The most important result of that visit and of his talks with Federal Chancellor Helmut Kohl is the agreement that the relationship between the two German states must remain a stabilizing factor for constructive East-West relations. Positive impulses for peaceful cooperation and dialogue in Europe and beyond must continue to emanate from that factor. The basic precondition for this is the recognition of the realities which have emerged as a result of postwar developments, in particular the existence of two sovereign German states independent of each other which are firmly anchored in their respective alliance systems.

To prevent all speculations or illusions may I add the words of our head of state: "We are far from having any pipedreams.... Socialism and capitalism are, as fire and water, incompatible with each other." Clarification in these areas was the prerequisite for laying down in a communiqué common positions and intentions regarding the cardinal question of our time, the safeguarding of peace, and for agreement on projects of further cooperation. In this sense, both states and peoples have gained by the visit, as have common sense and realism.

New thinking is a new approach to all questions concerning the coexistence of the two social systems in the world. I may inform you that the leading party of the German Democratic Republic, the Socialist Unity Party of Germany (SED), and the Social Democratic Party (SPD) in the Federal Republic of Germany recently adopted a joint document entitled "Conflicting Ideologies and Common Security." Both parties have come to the conclusion that the controversy between the two social systems can only take one form, the form of peaceful competition, of non-violent discussion concerning all political and ideological differences and of cooperation to their mutual benefit and advantage. In the process, both systems—irrespective of their fundamental socioeconomic, political, and ideological contradictions—must learn how to live with each other and get along well together.

The question of which social system is better should be answered and decided through peaceful competition. This means, *inter alia*, refraining from interfering in the internal affairs of the other side; refraining from arbitrarily dividing the world into "good and evil" and respective "empires" or stipulating "spheres of interest"; and letting the peoples decide in choosing their own social system. But it also means predictability, frankness, and restraint in the choice of means; the ability to carry on a dialogue, build confidence, reach consensus, reduce mistrust and fears, and collaborate on common tasks; and the elaboration of and agreement on a culture of political argument, rules of discussion and controversy.

Conclusion

In conclusion, permit me to state that the political and moral course of the new thinking is based on the mutual confidence of states and peoples, on respect for the dignity of man as well as for international institutions, and on the strict observance of all norms of international law. Through our policy of dialogue, understanding, and cooperation, we in the German Democratic Republic believe that we are rendering our own specific contribution to the solution of the global problems facing mankind. Together with our allies, friends, and partners we are ready to proceed from confidence-building measures in various fields to a large-scale policy of confidence which, step-by-step, will help establish the comprehensive system of international peace and security.

Let me end my presentation by quoting the great German writer Stefan Zweig. In his book *The Tide of Fortune* he writes: "Much that happens in history is indifferent and trivial.... It always takes millions of idle world hours before a truly historic moment of mankind appears." (Stefan Zweig called such a moment in German *Sternenstunde,* that is, "star hour.")

Let us work together so that this "star hour" is achieved and determinedly used everywhere—for peace on earth, and for eternal peace also for the stars.

America's Challenge to Gorbachev

by
John C. Whitehead
Deputy U.S. Secretary of State

I congratulate the Institute for East-West Security Studies and particularly its President, John Edwin Mroz, for all the constructive things it does, but particularly for its sponsorship of this highly successful conference. The Institute plays an increasingly effective role in bringing the East and West together through specific measures to clarify differences in perception, to stimulate new ideas for improving security, and to develop practical steps for building on shared concerns.

I particularly commend the Institute for its very excellent Report. It is interesting and encouraging that the panelists, who represent a very broad range of views, were able to agree on this quite specific statement. It indicates, I think, that a consensus is developing in the United States on how to deal with East-West relationships. And I must admit that my commendation of the Report is enhanced by the fact that its analysis and recommendations are generally very much in line with the policies of the administration.

I'm also very pleased to be with you in St. Paul today in such distinguished company. Your presence, and the conference's focus on "Soviet New Thinking," shows the keen interest we see today in examining what is fresh and new in the Soviet Union and in U.S.-Soviet relations. I share that interest, and the sense of excitement and hope that now goes with it, but my own focus this afternoon is somewhat different.

I want to suggest to you another way of looking at the reasons behind the recent progress in U.S.-Soviet relations that has aroused such expectations. The perspective I want to take puts more of a premium on *clear* thinking than on *"new"* thinking. That may be less romantic, perhaps, but it is also less likely to lead to exaggerated expectations which, if they are thwarted, would send U.S.-Soviet relations into a tailspin again. That is what happened toward the end of the last decade—another time when U.S.-Soviet relations were active and promising.

My subject today is "America's Challenge to Gorbachev." I chose it knowing full well that for the past two years the question has usually been put the other way around: how can America meet the challenge posed by a Soviet Union under new, dynamic leadership? As winds of change sprang up there, bringing promise of greater freedom and openness, and as Soviet officials moved with greater imagination and agility to advance their country's foreign policy interests, the critical question seemed to be how the United States should react. How should we shape our policies to take General Secretary Gorbachev's innovative domestic and international moves into account? Indeed, the title of the Institute's recent Report was "How Should America Respond to Gorbachev's Challenge?"

Now, to imply that the central question of U.S.-Soviet relations is how *we* should react to *Soviet* moves is bound to lead to a timid, reactive or unsteady U.S. policy. The central question should be: What are our interests? What is our agenda? That is the approach our government has taken, and I want to suggest to you that its success is a central reason for the surge of interest and hope of which this conference is just one reflection.

A Four-Part Challenge

My proposition is that much of what we find exciting in U.S.-Soviet relations just now can be seen as a Soviet response to America's challenge that it become a peaceful, constructive participant in the affairs of the modern world. The progress in our bilateral relations that we welcome is due as much to our steady pursuit of our central objectives in four key areas as it is to "new Soviet thinking."

One of the most promising things that has happened is that the Soviet leadership has agreed to work with us on the basis of the four-part agenda we believe is the only way to preserve balance in our relationship: human rights, arms control, regional conflicts, and bilateral issues. That in itself is a robust achievement. I will touch an all four of these areas later, but first let me make an observation on the relationship between the first two: human rights and arms control.

Human Rights and Arms Control

Most of you will recall the time—it was not more than a few years ago—when Soviet officials would dismiss any talk of human rights as blatant interference in their internal affairs. Indeed, they sometimes portrayed our raising of human rights issues with them as an attempt to sow obstacles in the way of arms control, which was pretty much all they wanted to talk about.

This is no longer the case today, and that is a change we welcome. On human rights, we now discuss Soviet laws and practices that we find troubling as well as the plight of individuals whose lives have been caught up in those practices. Not all the cases we raised have been resolved, nor have many outdated practices and laws yet been brought up to date. But there has been progress, and we welcome it. We think much more is needed, but we're glad to have a regular dialogue with Soviet leaders about human rights. That is the way we think modern countries should deal with issues in which they have a common interest, so the dialogue itself is a good sign in the perspective of our overall aims.

But two points need to be made here. First, the modest changes in Soviet human rights practices did not come at the expense of arms control, as some had warned. Indeed, as we have said for years, the impact of human rights issues on the possibility of arms control agreements really works the other way around. Increased Soviet respect for human rights enhances the prospects for an atmosphere where arms control agreements can be reached and ratified. The more closely the Soviet Union complies with its obligations under the Helsinki Final Act, the more credible a partner it becomes in arms control. This point is especially germane now, as we stand on the verge of a historic agreement to eliminate an entire class of nuclear weapons and when we are both committed to work toward a 50-percent cut in strategic weapons.

Second, it seems to me that we will be in a better position to elicit increased Soviet respect for human rights if we avoid being entranced by the novelty of what is happening in the

Soviet Union and keep in mind how much distance is left to be covered. If that seems to you an ungenerous attitude, I can only point out that it is based on the sobering experience of the 1970s, when a relaxation of U.S.-Soviet tensions on one level was accompanied by a methodical decimation of the independent Soviet human rights movement.

I hope and believe that the situation today is different. But until the improvements we have seen are secured by enduring changes in Soviet institutions, in law and in settled practice, a lively, regular, and persistent dialogue on human rights will remain at the top of our agenda with the Soviet leadership. Last week's news that Ida Nudel will be released was a gratifying event that surely would not have taken place without that dialogue.

So long as hundreds of thousands of Soviet Jews who wish to leave are unable to do so, so long as outdated laws and practices throw barriers between husbands and wives and between families and their loved ones, so long as restraints are placed on the free practice of religion and on political and artistic expression, there will be self-imposed limits to the Soviet Union's capacity to act as a full member of the international community, and to our ability to interact with the Soviet Union on a cooperative basis.

It is very important, I think, as we follow developments in the Soviet Union, to maintain a sober perspective and avoid exaggeration and wishful thinking. Too often in the past, America's perception of the Soviet Union has veered from visions of the millennium to scenes from the apocalypse, and our bilateral relations have soared and plunged on the same roller-coaster ride. That's bad for both countries, and I'm told it makes the rest of the world very nervous, too. So we want to avoid that, and to steer a steady course.

I think the United States is well placed to do that, but before I go on to explain why, let me make just a few remarks on how we see the changes taking place under General Secretary Gorbachev's leadership and how we relate to them.

The Anatomy of Soviet Reforms

The Soviet Union is a less inaccessible society today than in the recent past, but we are still far from understanding the reasons for the changes taking place there. Broadly speaking, though, it seems to us that after a period of economic, social, and political stagnation, the Soviet leadership decided that urgent steps are needed to ensure that the Soviet economy stays within hailing distance of other modern economies as the world moves further along into the age of high technology.

Upon becoming party leader in March 1985, Mr. Gorbachev first tried to accomplish this by what the Soviets call "acceleration," which amounts to trying to make the economy produce more goods and services faster, but without any fundamental changes in its structure or operation. This didn't work, and he went on to introduce in turn a set of other, more radical measures intended to get the sluggish economy moving. Their Russian names by now have a familiar ring to most of us:

- *perestroika*, or "reconstruction," which refers to steps such as increased decentralization and greater accountability;

- *glasnost'*, which means a less restricted public airing of ideas and information;

- and then *demokratizatsiia*, or "democratization," which sounds very good indeed but refers in practice to the introduction of certain steps, such as multiple candidates in some elections, to increase citizen interest and involvement in the political process.

How the Soviet leadership sees this loosening up—how far it will go and where it will lead—is the subject of much current speculation. We think it was originally introduced as a necessary means toward the goal of a more dynamic and creative economy, not as an end in itself. In other words, increased freedom of expression is considered good because it will make for a stronger, more innovative economy, not because it is a "right."

We understand that institutional and legal reforms are under study, but the steps that we have seen so far toward making the Soviet Union a more open and humane society remain vulnerable to arbitrary reversal. What rights their citizens enjoy are not yet inalienable by any government decree, as are the rights granted to Americans by the Constitution whose two-hundredth anniversary we celebrated this year. Similarly, it would be difficult to argue that the Soviet economy has yet been transformed in any permanent way.

How new are these internal developments? That, of course, depends on your point of view. I expect that those of you who are from Eastern Europe view Soviet "new thinking" with mixed emotions. Some of the economic steps now being debated in the USSR are recognizable as very similar to those already carried out some years ago in your countries. Or perhaps your thoughts return to the more fundamental strivings for reform, as in Hungary in 1956, Czechoslovakia in 1968, and most recently Poland, that were tragically brought to an abrupt end by the Soviet Union.

It may seem ironic to you that it is now the Soviet leader who is greeted as the champion of reform as he travels in Eastern Europe. That has certainly not been the rule in the past. An even more desirable innovation, it seems to us, would be the recognition that Soviet "new thinking" means the end of Soviet attempts to impose either reform *or* reaction on its East European neighbors, leaving them free to determine their own future and select their own road to get there.

But if Soviet experimentation does not look so new when compared to what has been done elsewhere, it nevertheless is new, striking, and significant when viewed against the background of Russian history. On that I want to be clear. It is not my intention to dismiss the changes taking place in the Soviet Union during the past two years as meaningless or irrelevant. On the contrary, we see them as promising and hopeful, even if their long-term effect is far from clear. Nor do we believe Mr. Gorbachev's program for change is purely rhetorical, although rhetoric and slogans play an important part in it.

What we are seeing is very much a program of reform from above, and one whose initiators have no intention of turning it into a movement for a multi-party, democratic political system. But that does not rob it of significance, both as a source of opportunities for us to advance our interests in a constructive way, and on its own terms, as a process that could and should take on a life of its own.

How this process of evolution will play itself out in the Soviet Union will probably be influenced more by internal factors than anything else, but not solely by them. As Soviet officials now regularly point out, we live in an interdependent world. What happens in Budapest or Beijing—or here in St. Paul, for that matter—is now increasingly likely to affect what happens in Moscow. Ideas make their way around the globe with the speed of light. As they do, I am confident that the influence of American values and ways of doing things will have a measurable impact on the direction Soviet society takes.

Challenge by Example

This is the other side of the American challenge. Earlier I spoke to you of the four-part agenda that we advance in our official dialogue with Soviet leaders. That is one challenge to Gorbachev: to work with us in specific ways in those four areas. But America also poses a challenge simply by its example, by being what it is: a remarkably open, dynamic, creative, and caring society. Like Russia's, our history is written on a large scale by peoples of many nationalities, and despite sharp divergences in the paths our societies have taken, the answers we in the United States have found to economic, social, and political problems are rich with potential for application elsewhere.

Is the question how to improve agricultural output? Our outstandingly productive farmers have set the standard for the world. In fact, the senior Soviet official responsible for agriculture, Politburo member Viktor Nikonov, is traveling around the United States right now, with a visit to Iowa set for this afternoon. We want him to see our achievements and our problems. If there is something useful to be learned, we would be delighted.

Do we want to determine whether a freer flow of ideas leads to increased creativity? Our open society, where the freedom to express one's views on anything under the sun is perhaps our most cherished constitutional right, is also a giant open laboratory for tracing the connection between the flow and clash of ideas and industrial or artistic innovation.

What are the merits of decentralization versus central control—in industry, in politics, in the arts? The American experience offers a wealth of evidence, we think, that a healthy measure of local individual autonomy is indispensable for a resilient economy, a responsible political system, and genuine artistic expression.

Most importantly, we offer our experience in shaping one complex but integral and vibrant society out of peoples from enormously diverse backgrounds and with different aspirations. The process has not been painless for us, it has not always gone smoothly or fairly, and it is far from over. But we think it holds evocative lessons for the way the social contract must be drawn up to yield a dynamic, productive society.

On all these questions, our ideas and experiences will reach the Soviet Union through the growing network of people-to-people contacts that is developing between us. I am confident our values will make an impact, just as we will take their ideas and interests into account.

Holding a Steady Course

I said earlier that I thought the United States is in a good position to avoid the highs and lows we are used to seeing in the U.S.-Soviet relationship. Let me tell you why by hazarding a view on what went wrong the last time we were in a period of expanding relations with the Soviet Union.

The policy of detente was framed at a time when the United States, bruised by its Vietnam involvement and the social unrest of the 1960s, appeared to face narrowing global options. The Soviet Union, on the other hand, enjoyed growing military and economic strength. The resulting U.S. policy was essentially defensive, intended to set up a process for managing adverse trends. It gave arms control a disproportionate role and, at a time when U.S. defense expenditures were stagnating, took the attitude that any limits on Soviet capabilities were better than none.

It has been the thesis of the Reagan administration that, *first*, the situation in which the United States found itself could be changed to our advantage, with the application of resources and resolve; and, *second*, our policy toward the Soviet Union must be assertive, not defensive, balanced, not restricted to arms control but extending to *all* the issues that arise when two competing great powers must live with each other on the same shrinking planet, and based on confidence in our strength, not a sense of relative decline.

This approach led directly to the four-part agenda with which you are familiar: human rights, arms control, regional problems, and bilateral issues. Progress in each area is pursued on its own merits, based on our definition of what we want and the Soviet definition of what they want. In that situation, negotiability is not the main criterion, but if agreements can be reached by negotiation, they are going to be agreements that benefit both sides.

We can now see the fruits of that policy. In *human rights,* the U.S. government no longer finds itself playing the apologist for Soviet human rights performance in order to protect other elements of the relationship from being damaged. Instead, we have vigorously advanced both individual cases and the need to adhere to international norms of conduct. I do not claim this is the sole reason for the improvement in Soviet performance, but it is certainly a contributing cause. As history has demonstrated, no other approach will be supported by the American people and Congress.

In *arms control,* no longer viewed as an end in itself, for the first time actual *reductions* in nuclear weapons are on the verge of being agreed upon. To avoid the kinds of Soviet violations that earlier agreements left room for, rigorous verification provisions will be built in.

Regional issues were the proximate cause of the unraveling of detente as the Soviet Union sought new footholds in Angola, Ethiopia and Afghanistan. These Soviet moves were perceived as violating a joint undertaking not to seek "unilateral advantage," which was the strongest block to Soviet adventurism we could mount at a time when the public and the Congress would not back a more vigorous defense of U.S. interests around the globe. As a result, the dream of a "new structure of peace" that was widely heralded in the early 1970s simply exploded, and the fallout damaged a number of very concrete accomplishments of that era.

With this lesson before it, the Reagan administration has proceeded with a conviction of the need for real commitment on the ground to protect U.S. interests. As a result, the costs of using military means to advance Soviet influence have risen, and there is evidence of a reappraisal of some past actions. In Afghanistan, the Soviets, while still dragging their feet on withdrawal, have tacitly admitted their intrusion was a failure. It remains for them to make the hard decisions which would terminate their involvement. In Angola, in Nicaragua, in

Cambodia, the fruits of apparent Soviet gains during the 1970s have turned increasingly bitter, and the world is learning the lesson that democracy's roots are strong when other democratic countries are prepared to nourish them.

Our more forthright policy on regional conflicts has made largely irrelevant divisive debates here about "linkage." Just as we deal with Soviet international conduct on its merits, so do we approach bilateral questions.

Each element of the *bilateral relationship* must stand on its own merits. The new framework of cooperative activities taking shape after the Geneva summit has been subjected to careful review, to ensure that the benefits are mutual. We are moving ahead on possible cooperation in areas such as transportation, basic sciences and maritime search and rescue, as well as a wealth of people-to-people exchanges. Progress may be slower than at some "boom" periods of U.S.-Soviet relations in the past because we are moving more carefully, but we would rather set a steady, even course than get back on the roller-coaster again.

Bipartisan Consensus

An important factor tending to keep U.S.-Soviet relations on a steady course, I think, is the growth of a bipartisan consensus in the United States, for the first time in decades, on how we should conduct the U.S.-Soviet relationship. This is the result of several factors. One is certainly the willingness of the Soviet leadership to apply some "new thinking" to some of the Cold War preconceptions that have guided their relations with the West for most of the postwar period. This certainly tends to make the Soviet Union a more promising partner.

Another reason, I believe, is the strong desire of those who have followed the ups and downs of the U.S.-Soviet drama—and by now, that means much of the American public—to stop the pendulum swings and settle down to relations based on strength, on commitment to peaceful solutions to problems, and on systematic dialogue. This would be grounded in the realistic sense that we are dealing with a country in many ways unlike us, but one with which we can have a stable if competitive relationship.

The Future

What could that relationship look like if the new elements in it develop and flourish in the coming years?

In late August, at the delightful Chautauqua town meeting with men and women from the Soviet Union that is becoming an annual affair, I pointed to a world, several decades in the future, in which we might live if everything works out for the very best. It would be a world from which the threat of nuclear holocaust has been lifted and U.S.-Soviet confrontation in the Third World is a thing of the past. Young American and Soviet citizens would visit each other's countries, study in each other's schools, fall in love and marry with only the complications that normally accompany love affairs, not the bureaucratic obstacles they now face. Our scientists, working together, would solve the energy problem with the creation of clean and safe fusion power.

That is a pleasant but distant dream. We can let it inspire us, but it is too soon to be certain that it is within our reach. In the more immediate future, we have to assume that a sharp element of competition will remain in U.S.-Soviet relations. We can, though, work to make sure that it is not the kind of deadly competition that brings us to the edge of Armageddon.

We can strive to reduce the extent to which national security concerns dominate the relationship by negotiating force reduction agreements, both nuclear and conventional. We can deepen our dialogue on human rights questions so that the suspicion which Soviet human rights practices have created over many years can be lifted. In that context, we can look toward the growth of trade toward the levels one might expect between two such huge economies. We can break down some more of the barriers to the movement of ideas and of people. We can work together to build a world that is far from perfect but a good deal safer, calmer, and more humane than the one we live in today.

Both worlds are worth working toward, and we are nearer to them than we were a decade ago. To reach them, we will need not only new thinking, but clear, realistic thinking, and fidelity to the principles that got us to the promising point we have reached today.

Conference Summary

The discussions in the various panels and working groups at the conference sought to address the main issue raised by the Institute's Task Force Report, *How Should America Respond to Gorbachev's Challenge?* While the views expressed reflected various cross sections of American, West European, and East European opinion, it was widely agreed that the Report represented an important contribution to the analysis of current Soviet domestic and foreign policy changes, and of the broader consequences of those changes for East-West relations. One of the central uncertainties raised by the Report—the significance of Gorbachev's personality and the durability of his tenure as general secretary of the CPSU—was the source of much debate throughout the conference. While most participants accepted the idea of the far-reaching character of Gorbachev's domestic reforms, they were less certain about their link to foreign policy and the kinds of responses called for from the international community. Many participants pointed to the need for a multilateral approach to the challenges and opportunities posed by contemporary Soviet policies, going beyond purely bilateral U.S.-Soviet steps to include allies and CSCE partners. This, they argued, had become more urgent in light of Gorbachev's September 17 *Pravda* article and recent indications of a shift in the Soviet attitude toward international organizations, particularly the United Nations. Many saw in this shift a hopeful sign that the USSR would take multilateral diplomacy more seriously in the future, and that the UN might therefore be able to play a more forceful role in helping to resolve international disputes.

The conference discussions tended to break down into five main topics: structural sources of change in Soviet policies; economic and social dimensions of the Soviet domestic reform; impact of Soviet policy on European security; the political and ideological competition; and crisis management.

1. Structural Sources of Change in Soviet Policies

A number of participants from West European countries felt that a potential weakness of the Report, as with much of Western opinion on current Soviet policy, was a tendency to place undue emphasis on the "Gorbachev factor." This question assumes particular significance after the resignation of Boris Yeltsin, a strong Gorbachev supporter, as Moscow party chief in early November. What would happen, they asked, if the general secretary's position should weaken? Was not the West placing too much emphasis on one person, whose views are far from being universally accepted in various segments of Soviet society?

Several experts from Eastern Europe and the United States argued forcefully that the changes taking place in the USSR could not be reduced to the personality factor, though they conceded that Gorbachev is key to the scope and pace of the reforms currently being undertaken. Two East European participants stressed the need for institutional changes in the socialist countries, noting that the crisis of economic stagnation could only be addressed effectively with social and even political reforms. No Soviet or East European leader could ignore, they said, the structural sources of economic stagnation. In the Soviet case, the international consequences of a progressive decline of the economy for the USSR would force any leader, whether Gorbachev or someone else, to reexamine basic operating assumptions.

Dr. Robert Legvold, Director of Columbia University's W. Averell Harriman Institute for Advanced Study of the Soviet Union, echoed these concerns. In a speech to the conference, Legvold said that the West has underestimated the extent of change in Soviet policies because it has misunderstood the systemic sources of the USSR's problems. Western observers were thus inclined to underrate the strength of Gorbachev's political position as well as the irreversibility of the reform program now being implemented. In support of this view, Legvold pointed to the convergence of two historical trends which have been percolating since Khrushchev's time: (1) the obsolescence of the Stalinist economic order, based on extensive economic production, at a time when conversion to intensive production is essential—by the late 1970s the USSR could no longer have simultaneous increases in consumption, civilian investment, and military production; and (2) a shift in the Stalinist social order, as the industrial working class gave way to the educated middle class as the key production factor in the Soviet economy. With two-thirds of the Soviet population now well educated and living in cities (compared to the reverse in the 1950s), a different social base with a need for a different "social compact" with the ruling elite has emerged in the USSR. The traditional Soviet social compact, in which basic social security and elemental needs were guaranteed by the state in exchange for acquiescence in tight control from the center, no longer moves the emerging classes in Soviet society. As a consequence, there has been increased recognition of conflicts of interest within the society; a shift from the notion of a "single truth" to recognizing the need for diversity of opinions on public issues; a retreat from utopia with strict limits to "social engineering"; and a shift from collectivism to recognition of greater individualism and social diversity. These deeply rooted social forces mean that change will continue independent of individual leaders, though perhaps in different forms and to a different extent than under Gorbachev. These were permanent factors, Legvold stressed.

Legvold suggested that there were a number of important factors beyond Gorbachev's or any Soviet leader's control in the shaping of Soviet foreign policy as well. He pointed to five such factors:

- The dynamism of the capitalist world, which has led to the information revolution and a growing economic gap with the East.

- The intractability of change in the Third World, together with the fact that since the late 1970s the USSR has found itself in the position of propping up threatened regimes in Angola, Afghanistan, Cambodia, etc.

- A structural shift in power relations in international politics, with a decrease in superpower influence, particularly within their own alliance systems.

- Greater interdependence, which refutes the purely "zero-sum" view of international relations and highlights the impact of forms of power other than armed forces.

- The consequences of nuclear parity: given the obvious limits to the political use of nuclear weapons, what kind of military policy should the USSR have under conditions of both a continuing arms race and nuclear parity?

Again, these factors would influence Soviet foreign policy even if Gorbachev were not at the helm. The central question is, would adjustments in Soviet thinking about world politics brought about by these external changes lead to changes in the guidelines for Soviet foreign policy in such key areas as security, international political order, change in the Third World, and relations with its socialist neighbors?

A specialist from the GDR addressed this question by arguing that the "new political thinking" in the East stems from the appreciation of "new facts," as he put it, which have led to a condition of "interdependence for survival." These include (1) the military threat to human survival represented by nuclear weapons; (2) the deterioration of ecological processes worldwide, also a "species threat"; (3) a widening and increasingly dangerous gap in levels of development between the Third World and the industrially advanced countries; and (4) the global, irreversible economic and social processes set in motion by the scientific-technological revolution. Both East and West are equally exposed to these processes, he said. The new thinking is thus not a mere tactical shift of course but a strategic imperative requiring multilateral steps to construct a "war-prevention regime" that would include an abandonment of deterrence as the basis of security policy and policies of active cooperation in the security, economic/ecological, and humanitarian fields.

2. Economic Reform and International Economic Policy

The discussion on Soviet (and by extension East European) economic reform and foreign economic policy was best captured by the observations of a Hungarian economist and a U.S. investment banker. The Soviet economic reform, the Hungarian expert stressed, is a deeply rooted process, aimed at transforming the Stalinist conception of the socialist economy and the socialist system. While effective change can only be gradual, Gorbachev has already made a good start, he felt; indeed, Gorbachev has gone farther than he originally intended. While there is much uncertainty about the reform process in the short run, in the long run the only effective course is for greater integration into the world economy. Special economic zones should be created throughout the Soviet and East European economies, he said, as in China, to accelerate the integration of select parts of their economies into the global market.

The crucial economic question, he felt, was how to survive the first three to five years of the reform. In social and political terms the key is not so much in importing capital or technology— the effects of which can only make themselves felt in the long run—but how to provide some sort of tangible reward to the general population until the necessary transition period passes. Other problems that the USSR and the other socialist countries will have to face, as the Hungarian reform experience shows, involve the ideological and institutional aspects of economic reform. In order to use effectively the technology already in their possession, the socialist economies will have to make far-reaching changes in their social structures and practices. This touches upon central elements of the social-political systems in these countries, such as egalitarianism in wage distribution. A more differentiated income scale would certainly lead, at least temporarily, to a rise in social tensions. Basic reforms of political institutions are thus also essential, he said: a reform that is managed from above can only have a partial and less than optimal impact.

U.S. participants generally agreed with this analysis. One analyst, whose views reflected the U.S. consensus, stressed that the economic changes now underway or being planned in the USSR pose both opportunities and risks for the West. It will, he felt, become progressively more difficult for Gorbachev to implement the reform, which requires far-reaching changes in the pricing system and in the role of the party in managing the economy. Nevertheless, for the foreseeable future Gorbachev clearly wants to redirect some military resources to other areas of the economy, in order to modernize the basic economic infrastructure and equipment (civilian investment) and provide greater individual and social amenities for a population in search of meaningful material incentives (consumption). Over time, a strengthened civilian economic structure, with a more decentralized and open modus operandi, could reduce the military's preeminent claim upon resources. He also noted that the USSR has expressed a strong interest in international economic contacts on all levels. At the same time, there is presently little constituency within the USSR that sees Western technology imports as substitutes for meaningful reform (as was the case in the early 1970s). Without reform, technology cannot be efficiently used.

How should the West respond to this situation? The U.S. participant felt that both the opportunities and the risks of the Soviet reform process should be carefully taken into account. Among the opportunities he listed the following:

- The military will be unable to redirect resources to itself suddenly.

- Larger numbers of influential Soviets will be exposed to the West—this could reduce the Soviet sense of isolation, provide reassurances about Western intentions, and strengthen the constituency in the USSR in favor of restraint in foreign and military policy.

- There will be greater opportunities for Western exports to the USSR (especially of equipment).

Among the risks he mentioned:

- A tendency in the United States to misunderstand the nature of the linkages between political and economic relations: the United States should not overestimate the leverage it possesses and should be consistent in its linkage policy.

- The danger of unilateral U.S. action on key East-West trade issues, leading to friction within the Atlantic alliance.

- The current absence of any "economic verification" process. It is essential that there be greater predictability in East-West trade ties, and thus greater information available about actual economic practices in the USSR.

While the speaker underscored the limits of Western influence on Soviet domestic policy, he concluded that the West should increase the level of contacts with the USSR and Eastern Europe on all levels, including the economic one, which would increase the predictability and consistency of economic interchanges between East and West, and thereby reinforce the tendencies toward moderation in the application of Soviet power.

3. Impact on European Security

A major topic of discussion was the impact of a major withdrawal of medium- and short-range missiles on European security. West European participants stressed caution in moving too rapidly from an agreement on INF forces to other areas of arms control. They were very concerned about the tendency toward denuclearization of security on the continent and the new importance of the conventional balance, which in their view decidedly favors the USSR. They stressed that in many ways conventional force issues are even more complicated to negotiate than nuclear ones, since the key issue is not numbers per se but the stability of the balance of forces. This stability, they said, is a consequence of force structures, doctrines, and intentions, in addition to simple numbers of forces. The geographic disparity between the two alliances—with the United States lying an ocean apart—would also have to be taken into account in new conventional force talks.

French participants in particular reinforced this skepticism, arguing that Gorbachev's "new political thinking" did not include any move toward self-determination for the peoples of Eastern Europe—in their view a central purpose of detente—and that efforts to devalue nuclear deterrence in Europe could be destabilizing both politically and militarily. There was a strong consensus among NATO-country participants that nuclear systems should not be included in new conventional force talks, though functionally related systems—such as the West's nuclear artillery versus the East's forward-based armor—might be discussed.

East European participants did not share this view. They stressed that the INF accord—the first to envisage the elimination of an entire weapons system—was seen as only the first stage of what they termed a "comprehensive" approach to East-West and global security, encompassing the eventual abolition of nuclear weapons as well as political and economic confidence-building measures. A Polish specialist made the case for a single forum to deal with both conventional and nuclear force issues—a suggestion which was rejected by British and French participants—and raised the possibility of a nuclear- and other weapons-free corridors in central Europe, the discussion of operational military doctrines on an alliance-to-alliance basis, asymmetrical force reductions on both sides, and a code of conduct regulating international disputes.

An expert from the German Democratic Republic rejected the cautionary attitude of many Western participants, noting the political significance of the INF accord, which "would furnish practical proof that it is possible to bring about more security and confidence through political accords and agreements." Such an agreement, he said, "must be followed by further agreements." He mentioned the following steps as essential:

- the reduction of tactical nuclear weapons, including battlefield nuclear systems;

- the radical reduction of offensive strategic weapons while strengthening the regime of the ABM Treaty;

- a comprehensive nuclear test-ban treaty;

- a convention abolishing chemical weapons;

- the reduction of conventional forces in Europe to the point where each side possesses only a defensive capability, in which surprise attack would be impossible;

- a nuclear weapons-free corridor in central Europe, leading to a reduction of forward-based offensive conventional units;

- the acceptance of the principle of asymmetrical force reductions and strict verification provisions; and

- improved political relations, including those between the German Democratic Republic and the Federal Republic of Germany.

U.S. and West European participants were skeptical as to the substance and desirability of many of the Eastern proposals. While both sides appeared at times to be speaking the same vocabulary, the operational meaning of such key terms as doctrine, surprise attack capability, and asymmetrical cuts (not to mention the hardy perennial, i.e., the statistics of the existing force balance) remained to be defined.

When challenged by the GDR participant to specify the kinds of measures needed to rectify existing (perceived) imbalances and to change capabilities, a U.S. official, speaking in his personal capacity, mentioned two foci of Western concern: (1) the ability to launch a surprise attack with forces-in-being or readily mobilized; and (2) the capability for sustained offensive operations on a potential opponent's territory. This meant, at a minimum, no increased force commitments in the key central European area and, secondly, stability measures that would reduce and limit the operations of forward-based attack equipment. There would be collective ceilings at the lowest possible levels, with simultaneous exchanges of information between the sides before and during the implementation of the accord. There would have to be stringent verification, he said, which meant the withdrawal of entire units (which leave identifiable "signatures," as partial withdrawals do not). Given the geographic asymmetries involved, the United States would have to have prepositioned weapons stockpiles in Europe. Furthermore, reductions would have to be very asymmetrical—NATO studies have shown that asymmetrical withdrawals of forward-based armor units on the order of 4:1 or 5:1 would have to take place in order to leave the West in a condition of equal or improved security at lower levels of arms.

A GDR participant strongly contested the American's assumptions about the existing force balance in Europe, which suggested that the group was receiving a foretaste of the difficulty of negotiations on conventional force issues. Behind all of the dicussion and debate, one thing seemed clear: the attitude toward proposals for arms control and changes in the political-military order in Europe depended strongly on the vision of the future of Europe. Discussions about force levels and arms control are often a surrogate for the deeper issue of the political meaning of Europe and European security.

4. The Political and Ideological Competition

Another major focal point of discussion was the political and ideological competition between East and West. The discussion addressed a number of key questions:

- What is the relationship between the political and ideological competition between the USSR and the West?

- How does the ideological factor enter into the new Soviet political thinking in foreign policy?

- What are the implications of this new thinking for such issues as the Third World, Eastern Europe, and, in particular, Afghanistan?

There was a general consensus among the Western participants on five propositions. *First,* as Gorbachev changes the language by which the USSR deals with its relations with other nations (e.g., "mutal security" and new nuances to "peaceful coexistence"), the West will have to determine which terms represent mere lexical changes in what remains traditional Soviet ideology and which signify important shifts in the way the USSR conducts the competition with the West. While this language is still in flux, it is essential to understand it.

Second, while it is premature to say that this new vocabulary and style have significantly changed the overall nature and danger of the political competition, there are strong indications that there has been a genuine Soviet appreciation of interdependence in its foreign relations and a somewhat greater application of multilateralism in approaches to regional conflicts. In such key areas as Afghanistan, the Iran-Iraq war, and even the Arab-Israeli conflict, the USSR has moved away from its traditional bilateral, superpower-focused approach to security and countenanced a greater role for the United Nations, regional actors, and, in principle, the International Court of Justice.

Third, the major area in which the political competition will continue to occur is the issue of human rights. Respect for human rights and fundamental freedoms, as well as the freer flow of information and people guaranteed by the Helsinki Accords, will continue to be a touchstone of progress in East-West relations and an area in which the West should continue to pressure Moscow to observe its assumed international obligations. A human rights conference in Moscow could be considered if the USSR agrees to free entry to the conference from all interested parties and guarantees their freedom of movement, access to the Soviet population, and free transmission of information.

Fourth, Eastern Europe remains the most critical and controversial area where the Soviet approach to the political competition will be tested, as Gorbachev's reforms are developed in each of the East European nations in different ways. Peaceful political, economic, and social change in Eastern Europe which leads to the fulfillment of those nations' national interests along the lines of the Helsinki Accords could change the shape of Europe and be a powerful force for peace and stability. Soviet reaction to change in Eastern Europe will say much about the extent to which the role of ideology has been modified in Soviet security calculations.

Finally, the East-West political competition in regional conflicts continues to have an incendiary potential for East-West relations. Any easing of the intensity of this competition can come only after intensive superpower efforts to define their respective interests and the security issues involved in each case. Yet ultimately, fundamental change in this competition will depend on the extent to which the USSR reduces its commitment to support violent revolution outside its borders and "national liberation" movements. While there are signs that the USSR has been reevaluating the costs and benefits of political-military expansionism in the Third World, it was not yet clear whether this signified a traditional "consolidation" period or a fundamental change of attitude.

These five points, Western participants felt, should be on the agenda of every U.S.-Soviet summit meeting.

Eastern participants forcefully presented their own views of the link between current Soviet policies and the political-ideological competition. Several Eastern discussants underscored Robert Legvold's emphasis on the structural sources of change in the USSR. They stressed that the changes currently observable in Soviet domestic and foreign policy reflect deeply rooted systemic trends and that these trends would continue (although their pace and scope might differ) independent of the identity of the Soviet leader. One Eastern participant said that economic changes were already visible in the USSR during Khrushchev's time, but that they had failed due to the absence of corresponding social reforms. The fact that Gorbachev understands the social foundations of effective economic reform in the USSR means that the reform can be successful.

At the same time, he continued, even social reforms are not enough; institutional changes affecting the patterns of political power are also needed. This does not mean, however, that there has been any deemphasis on ideology, as one Western participant had argued. On the contrary, the East European specialist said, Soviet society currently possesses an institutional framework that is based on explicitly ideological values, which give legitimacy to the system and its leaders. The reforms now being introduced in the USSR are presented as a continuation of the deeper, Leninist Soviet tradition. To buttress the case for reform, the regime must clothe it in the legitimating ideology. The ideological imprint is further reinforced by the fact that Soviet patriotism itself is heavily informed by the socialist vision. Thus, ideology, reform, and patriotism are closely interwined, providing the foundation of legitimacy that is an "obsession" with the Soviet leadership. In the end, he said, it would be a serious mistake to underrate the continuing impact of ideology in Soviet politics and foreign policy: Soviet ideology is still closely related to deeply held socialist beliefs.

In conclusion, East European participants cautioned against a mechanistic interpretation of the specific impact of ideology on Soviet policies. Gorbachev has explicitly stated (most recently in a key article printed in *Pravda* on September 17, 1987) that the new political thinking involves national security affairs as well. This is to include an approach to military policy which emphasizes defensive over offensive forces; indeed, there has begun a reinterpretation of the military history of World War II designed to highlight the intrinsic advantages of the defense, a novel development in Soviet military thinking. There also appears to have been a reevaluation of the Soviet attitude to Third World conflicts, with the conclusion that the USSR should avoid overextending itself—due to dubious prospects for success, open-ended claims upon scarce Soviet resources, and the negative impact upon East-West relations.

5. Impact on Crisis Management

Those taking part in the discussion on the impact of Gorbachev's policy on crisis prevention and management took strong issue with the contention of one participant that Gorbachev's leadership as such could add a highly destabilizing element to great-power relationships. Most agreed that the reinvigoration of the Soviet foreign policy apparatus was leading to a more creative Soviet diplomacy; this did not, in their view, make that diplomacy more dangerous. Secondly, as one Polish observer put it, there is no indication that Gorbachev, while *primus inter pares*, does not have to answer to a collective leadership in the Politburo. Cautious, consensus politics is thus likely to prevail in crisis situations, much in the traditional pattern of Soviet diplomacy.

One U.S. participant drew a distinction between a "ripening" crisis, resulting from the pursuit by the USSR of long-standing objectives, and a crisis that has erupted suddenly, as a result of third-country activities. He felt that the new Soviet political thinking described in the Task Force's report could well affect Gorbachev's calculations of the risks involved in some of his long-term policies and thus may reduce the incidence of long-ripening crises, such as those over Berlin in the 1950s-1960s.

As for sudden crises, the impact of Gorbachev's new approaches seemed less clear, and the participant offered a three-part program. For the *present*, the USSR should discuss candidly with the United States outstanding differences on regional issues. For the *future*, both countries should work out general "rules of conduct" of acceptable international behavior that could be applicable to such crisis hot spots as the Iran-Iraq war. *Finally*, the Soviets should themselves undertake a critical analysis of the "old thinking," and examine the ways in which the USSR has made the United States feel insecure in the past.

Several discussants agreed that the Soviets are now interested in providing institutional arrangements that would help contain or resolve existing crises, and noted the references to strengthening the UN Security Council and peacekeeping forces made in Gorbachev's September 17 *Pravda* article. The apparent Soviet conviction that it is currently overextended in its foreign commitments may lead to fewer regional crises in the future, one participant added.

Participants generally agreed that the United States should proceed boldly to lock into place *now* procedures, methods, and institutions for crisis prevention and management. This would include crisis management centers, joint war rooms, improved military-to-military information exchanges and other confidence-building measures (CBMs). Opportunities currently exist for concluding a wide range of such CBMs that a subsequent Soviet leader would find difficult if not impossible to repudiate.

Finally, participants agreed that it is possible to work out rules of conduct in the U.S.-Soviet relationship, both for bilateral strategic relations and for superpower regional conduct. They cited the 1972 Incidents-at-Sea Agreement and the U.S.-Soviet Standing Consultative Commission on treaty compliance as workable models for future agreements and institutions that could help reduce the risks of war. In any case, as nuclear arms reductions are pursued, both sides must take care that crisis stability on the strategic nuclear and conventional levels—above all, maintaining strong disincentives to preemption—be maintained and even strengthened.

Conclusion

The discussions in St. Paul as a whole tended to confirm the basic thrust of the Task Force Report: that in the light of far-reaching and deeply rooted changes in Soviet domestic and foreign policies, the Western countries need to react creatively and reexamine some of their own policy assumptions. They should test the seriousness of Soviet initiatives by encouraging the USSR to continue developing negotiable proposals and practical approaches to issues of common security. At the same time, the West should be prepared to consider the practical consequences of its own declared policies, and to advance more creative initiatives. As the Task Force Report summed up: "New political thinking in the East requires new policy thinking in the West."

Executive Summary of the Task Force Report on Soviet New Thinking

Key Findings

In the face of domestic economic stagnation, widespread social apathy, and a widening technological gap vis-à-vis the West, Soviet General Secretary Mikhail Gorbachev has undertaken the most far-reaching revamping of the Soviet system in over half a century. While the Soviet Union remains a closed communist society, Gorbachev has challenged a whole series of ingrained practices and attitudes, from strictly centralized economic management to an often militarized foreign policy, which has been the basis for Soviet policy since Stalin's time. In foreign affairs, he has introduced new concepts and new flexibility into Soviet diplomacy. Yet the West has not come to terms with these changes.

Balancing Soviet power and maintaining a strong Western alliance remain central to U.S. national interests. By the same token, the U.S. and its allies have a long-term interest in encouraging the moderation of Soviet power. Because the Soviet Union is a global power, Gorbachev's initiatives demand an active response by the United States and its Western allies. In many areas, from arms control to emigration, the Soviet Union has begun to make changes in directions long advocated by the West. While far from complete, these changes present new opportunities, and challenges, which the West should not ignore. The Task Force strongly recommends that the United States and its Western allies welcome the reformist tendencies that Gorbachev has set in motion and encourage those which promote a moderation of Soviet power. Toward that end, the U.S. and its allies should engage the Soviet Union in an effort to explore possibilities for agreement and resolve key points of tension.

A purely reactive Western approach in the face of the new Soviet policy is not an acceptable option, the Task Force believes. Western policies as well as Gorbachev's domestic policy priority are bound to affect Soviet foreign policy. There is considerable uncertainty about the long-term success of Gorbachev's reforms. Nevertheless, over time, the new course chosen by Gorbachev will affect the ways in which the Soviet Union carries out its role as a superpower. A more subtle and flexible Soviet diplomacy requires the West to develop a broader and more active policy toward the Soviet Union, including standards to define and meet common security requirements in a rapidly changing international environment. Failure to do so would sacrifice the diplomatic initiative to the Soviet Union as well as abdicate our responsibility to future generations to pursue prospects for substantially improving relations between East and West.

What is Changing in Soviet Foreign and Domestic Policy?

The West needs to think anew about specific changes the Soviet Union has made in its own policies. Many of these changes are only beginnings and ultimate Soviet intentions remain unclear, but it is important to note that some of them move toward long-standing Western preferences:

- *Arms Control* — The USSR adopted the Western proposal of a zero option on the INF issue. In addition, the USSR has moved toward the Western positions on verification, including on-site inspection. It has also raised the prospect of asymmetrical conventional force reductions in central Europe. It has accepted the principle of deep reductions in offensive strategic weapons and proposed a concept of "sufficiency" in military forces.

- *Role of the Military* — There has been a reduction in the Soviet military's role and influence in the highest policy-making councils, and Gorbachev has made clear to the military that they have to accept spending restraints and greater openness in the dissemination of military information.

- *The International Economy* — Gorbachev has placed special emphasis on reducing Soviet autarky by increasing trade, joint ventures, and expressing an interest in cooperating with such major international organizations as GATT.

- *The Domestic Economy* — Gorbachev has initiated a major decentralization of operational responsibility for the economy, and he clearly intends to move toward a more flexible, modern, and efficient economic planning and management. He has admitted the inadequacy of Soviet statistics and called for more accurate economic information.

- *Human Rights* — In the fields of culture and dissent, Gorbachev has displayed a degree of openness and toleration unthinkable just three years ago. In the area of emigration, the change has been less dramatic but Gorbachev has increased the emigration of Soviet Jews, Germans and other groups. While *glasnost'* has a long way to go, it has clearly led to progress on human rights, which has been a major concern of the West.

- *Regional Issues* — While Gorbachev has as yet made no significant effort to scale back existing Soviet global commitments, he has given a lower priority to the military expansion of Soviet interests in the Third World than his predecessors.

- *Eastern Europe* — While urging closer and more "efficient" economic integration, Gorbachev has permitted a somewhat more flexible expression of specific national interests in Eastern Europe than his predecessors.

Agenda for Action

These changes in Soviet policies and the prospect of a Soviet-American INF treaty and summit by the end of this year highlight the need to tackle a wide range of problems in East-West relations. The Task Force recommends that as first steps Western policy choices focus on five key areas:

- *Security Issues* — The U.S. and its NATO allies should intensify talks with the Warsaw Pact aimed at reducing conventional forces and eliminating offensive strike potentials, particularly those designed for surprise attack.

Given the geographical differences and existing force imbalances, new approaches must include asymmetrical reductions of forward-based armored units, which present the greatest threat of surprise attack.

Both sides need to move rapidly to conclude an agreement on deep cuts in strategic offensive nuclear forces. These reductions should be designed to enhance strategic stability and eliminate the capacity to launch a crippling first strike. At the same time, both sides need to find ways to strengthen the ABM Treaty and to ensure that any research on strategic defensive systems is consistent with preservation of the Treaty.

The West should push for a rapid conclusion of the global Geneva chemical weapons negotiations, including the establishment of an international verification regime. Such an agreement would help increase confidence in Europe at a time when some are concerned over the implications of the elimination of medium- and shorter-range nuclear missiles from the continent.

- *International Economic Issues* — Except in a precisely defined area of strategic technologies, which entails tighter, more efficient COCOM regulations, expanded East-West trade is in our interest. The West should welcome Soviet efforts to develop the legal foundation for a system of equitable joint ventures. While Western governments should not subsidize credits, neither should they oppose the extension of private credit through normal commercial rates and practices to the Soviet Union. The prospect of observer status in the GATT and IMF should be used to encourage greater openness and information about the Soviet economy.

If the Soviet Union demonstrates heightened respect for human rights, the U.S. government and Congress should consider bringing their policy in congruence with U.S. allies by reevaluating the Jackson-Vanik and Stevenson amendments restricting trade with and credit to the USSR. The West should aim to normalize the framework for trade with all Warsaw Treaty countries, on the basis of mutual and reciprocal interests.

In addition, the U.S.-Soviet umbrella agreements on

scientific and technological cooperation should be revived and expanded, on the basis of full reciprocity.

- *Human Rights* — The West should welcome increased *glasnost'* while continuing to make clear to the Soviet government that its observance of internationally recognized human rights is the mark of a civilized power and a condition for truly collaborative relations between the Soviet Union and the West. The West should insist that the Soviet Union fully live up to the commitments it undertook under the Helsinki Final Act to encourage the freer movement of people, ideas, and information across international boundaries.

- *Regional Issues* — In Afghanistan, the West must continue to make clear that Soviet occupation of that country poses strict limits to genuine collaboration between the USSR and the West. Conversely, a rapid Soviet withdrawal, with sufficient international guarantees, would be a forceful demonstration that the "new political thinking" has specific policy implications.

  In other areas of conflict which could lead to possible superpower confrontation—such as Central America, southern Africa, and the Persian Gulf—the West should intensify discussions aimed at clarifying interests and creating conditions for greater stability. Within this framework, U.S.-Soviet meetings on regional issues should be upgraded as part of a regularized summit process. The purpose would be to seek solutions to these problems in conjunction with other concerned parties.

  In the Arab-Israeli dispute, the U.S. and USSR should work together to advance a peace process which guarantees the territorial integrity and interests of all states and parties.

- *Political Dialogue* — U.S.-Soviet summit meetings, as well as meetings at other governmental and non-governmental levels, should be held on a regular basis.

Conclusion

The West must have no illusions about the need to balance Soviet power, but neither should it overlook opportunities to encourage the Soviet Union to be a more responsible and integrated member of the international community. Although the long-term success of Gorbachev's policy remains uncertain, the process he has launched holds out a promise of a further moderation of Soviet power and an opportunity to develop and institutionalize areas of cooperation in the East-West relationship. Some in the West worry about giving the Soviet Union a "breathing spell. " They fear that Gorbachev's economic reforms will simply strengthen the USSR in the long run. But Soviet economic and social problems will not be quickly solved. In the meantime, greater openness and pluralization should be welcomed for their own sake as well as for the effect they can have in moderating the way Soviet power is used.

In order to seize the opportunities offered by new Soviet policies, the U.S. and its allies need to respond creatively to Gorbachev's initiatives. In order to do that, the West must be clear about its own policy objectives and priorities. New political thinking in the East requires new policy thinking in the West.

Speakers and Panelists
"The Implications of Soviet New Thinking"
October 9-11, 1987

Ivan T. Berend
Hungarian Academy of Sciences

Michael Binyon
The Times (London)

Bill Bradley
United States Senator

James Chace
Carnegie Endowment for International Peace

Philippe Coste
Ministry of External Relations, France

Kenneth W. Dam
Former U.S. Deputy Secretary of State

Thomas Downey
United States Congress

Bill Frenzel
United States Congress

Curt Gasteyger
Graduate Institute of International Studies (Geneva)

Robert Gavin
Macalester College

Hans-Dietrich Genscher
Minister of Foreign Affairs, FRG

James Giffen
U.S.-USSR Trade & Economic Council

Marshall Goldman
Harvard University Russian Research Center

David Gore-Booth
Foreign & Commonwealth Office, UK

Jon Gundersen
U.S. Arms Control & Disarmament Agency

John Hardt
Congressional Research Service

Steingrimur Hermannsson
Minister of Foreign Affairs, Iceland

Ed Hewett
The Brookings Institution

Robert Hormats
Goldman, Sachs and Co.

David Ignatius
The Washington Post

Donald Kendall
PepsiCo, Inc.

George Latimer
Mayor of St. Paul

Robert Legvold
W. Averell Harriman Institute for Advanced Study of the Soviet
 Union, Columbia University

Flora Lewis
The New York Times

William Luers
Metropolitian Museum of Art

Whitney MacMillan
Cargill, Inc.

Walter F. Mondale
Former Vice President of the United States

Ed Mortimer
Financial Times

Sam Nakagama
Nakagama & Wallace

Joseph Nye
Harvard University Center for Science & International Affairs

Harry Ott
Deputy Minister for Foreign Affairs, GDR

Roger Parkinson
Star Tribune (St. Paul)

William Pfaff
The Los Angeles Times

Helmut Sonnenfeldt
The Brookings Institution

Gary Stern
Federal Reserve Bank of Minneapolis

Thorvald Stoltenberg
Minister of Foreign Affairs, Norway

Michel Tatu
Le Monde

William Taubman
Amherst College

Richard Ullman
Princeton University

John C. Whitehead
U.S. Deputy Secretary of State